The Rise and Evolution of Bitcoin:

An Artistic Guide For Beginners to Experts

By Pashalis Laoutaris

Disclaimer

The Rise and Evolution of Bitcoin: An Artistic Approach

© 2024 by Pashalis Laoutaris. All rights reserved.

Cover and Interior Design by: Pashalis Laoutaris

First Edition: 04/2023

No part of this book may be used or reproduced in any manner whatsoever without written permission except in the case of brief quotations embodied in critical articles and reviews.

The information provided in this book is for informational purposes only and is not intended to be a source of advice or credit analysis concerning the material presented. The information and/or documents contained in this book do not constitute legal or financial advice and should never be used without first consulting with a financial professional to determine what may be best for your individual needs.

The publisher and the author do not make any guarantee or other promise as to any results that may be obtained from using the content of this book. You should never make any investment decision without first consulting with your financial advisor and conducting your own research and due diligence. To the maximum extent permitted by law, the publisher and the author disclaim any liability in the event any information, commentary, analysis, opinions, advice, and/or recommendations contained in this book prove to be inaccurate, incomplete or unreliable, or result in any investment or other losses.

Content contained or made available through this book is not intended to and does not constitute legal advice or investment advice and no attorney-client relationship is formed. The publisher and the author are providing this book and its contents on an "as is" basis. Your use of the information in this book is at your own risk.

For information contact laoutarisp@gmail.com

Table of Contents

Introduction
Chapter 1
    The Genesis of Bitcoin: Origins and Early Development
Chapter 2
    Early Adopters and Pioneers
Chapter 3
    The Emergence of Bitcoin Mining: From CPU to ASIC
Chapter 4
    Bitcoin Goes Mainstream: Its Rise to Prominence
Chapter 5
    The Technology Behind Bitcoin
Chapter 6
    The Future of Blockchain Technology
Chapter 7
    Challenges and Criticisms of Bitcoin
Chapter 8
    Regulatory Landscape for Bitcoin
Chapter 9
    Bitcoin's Competitors: The Rise of Alternative Cryptocurrencies
Chapter 10
    Future of Bitcoin
Chapter 11
    Risks and Challenges of Bitcoin

Chapter 12
- The Future of Bitcoin in Financial Systems

Chapter 13
- Investing in Bitcoin

Chapter 14
- Bitcoin's Ripple Effect: Impact on Society and Global Economy

Chapter 15
- Bitcoin's Dark Underbelly: Navigating the Shadows

Chapter 16
- The Forks and the Community Divide, starring Bitcoin and its progeny, Bitcoin Cash.

Chapter 17
- The Diverse Landscape of Cryptocurrency: Beyond Bitcoin's Horizon

Chapter 18
- Navigating the Legal Labyrinth: Bitcoin and Regulatory Realities

Chapter 19
- Bitcoin and Blockchain: A Dance of Technological Titans

Chapter 20
- Bitcoin and Political Ideals: A Canvas of Libertarianism, Anarchism, and More

Chapter 21
- Bitcoin's Dual Persona: Currency or Store of Value?

Chapter 22
- Bitcoin's Embrace: Fostering Financial Inclusion in the Developing World

Chapter 23
- Bitcoin Wallets: Varieties and Operations

Chapter 24
>   Bitcoin's Cultural Resonance

Chapter 25
>   Bitcoin Software Infrastructure

Chapter 26
>   The Blockchain: Verifying and Recording Bitcoin Transactions

Chapter 27
>   Bitcoin Trading: How to Buy and Sell Bitcoins

Chapter 28
>   Bitcoin's Market Volatility: What Causes It and How to Navigate It

Chapter 29
>   Approval of Bitcoin ETFs by the SEC

Chapter 30
>   Bitcoin and Cryptocurrency Innovations: What Lies Ahead?

Glossary

References

Introduction

Emerging in 2009 [1], Bitcoin, an innovative digital currency, has captured worldwide intrigue for its potential to reshape financial paradigms. Its fifteen-year-long odyssey paints a vivid backdrop of historical context, pivotal milestones, and profound ramifications.

The elusive visionary, or cabal of innovators, concealing their identity behind the pseudonym "Satoshi Nakamoto,"[2] unleashed Bitcoin upon the world through a cryptographic manifesto. This audacious proposition aimed to create an electronic peer-to-peer currency emancipated from the shackles of centralized authorities and intermediaries.

Bitcoin's foundational architecture [3] intertwines ingenious cryptographic techniques, a decentralized network fortified by an immutable distributed ledger, and an incentive mechanism fueling its propagation. Its blockchain backbone, an unbreakable chain of encrypted data blocks, safeguards the integrity and transparency of transactions, fostering an unprecedented paradigm of digital trust.

This tome delves into the intricate evolution of Bitcoin, mapping its modest inception to its ascent as a global marvel. The narrative unravels the endeavors of trailblazers, pivotal junctures, and technological leaps that propelled it into the spotlight while dissecting its societal and economic repercussions. From the inaugural Bitcoin transaction [4] to the rise of mining collectives and the advent of institutional investment, we chronicle the odyssey that transformed a disruptive concept into a mainstream phenomenon.

The chronicles of Bitcoin are indelibly intertwined with the turbulent undercurrents of the global financial landscape. Its emergence during the throes of the 2008 financial crisis marked [5] a poignant rebuke to the frailties of traditional monetary systems. As skepticism towards centralized financial authorities mounted, Bitcoin's decentralized ethos resonated with a burgeoning counterculture seeking an alternative path to economic emancipation.

Furthermore, we probe the obstacles and prospects ahead, acknowledging Bitcoin's potential to metamorphose conventional financial infrastructures. The discourse encompasses regulatory quandaries, environmental sustainability concerns, and the perpetual tussle between anonymity and oversight. Yet, amid these challenges, the promise of Bitcoin's underlying blockchain technology beckons a plethora of revolutionary applications across diverse sectors, from supply chain management to identity verification and beyond.

This opus extends an impartial and thorough scrutiny of Bitcoin, accentuating its virtues and limitations. We traverse the intricate dialogues encircling Bitcoin, from its libertarian origins to its capacity to nurture financial inclusiveness and societal advancement. Through a tapestry of perspectives, we unravel the multifaceted debates surrounding its status as a viable currency, a store of value, or a speculative asset.

Whether you're a seasoned cryptocurrency enthusiast or a curious neophyte, this tome aspires to furnish you with a comprehensive comprehension of Bitcoin and its intricate chronicle. Join us on this odyssey as we unravel the complexities and triumphs of this pioneering digital phenomenon, a harbinger of a technological renaissance poised to redefine the global financial landscape [6].

1. https://bitcoin.org/en/posts/ten-year-anniversary
2. https://www.britannica.com/biography/Satoshi-Nakamoto
3. https://bitcoin.org/bitcoin.pdf
4. https://www.nasdaq.com/articles/remembering-hal-finney-on-the-14th-anniversary-of-the-first-bitcoin-transaction
5. https://www.investopedia.com/articles/economics/09/financial-crisis-review.asp

6. https://www.imf.org/en/News/Articles/2024/02/23/sp022324-changing-landscape-crypto-assets-considerations-regulatory-and-supervisory-authorities

Chapter 1

The Genesis of Bitcoin: Origins and Early Development

Conceived from a vision of a decentralized digital currency, Bitcoin aimed to circumvent conventional financial intermediaries, reinstating control to its users. Its origins trace back to a 2008 white paper authored under the pseudonym Satoshi Nakamoto by an enigmatic individual or collective whose true identity remains shrouded in mystery to this day.

Entitled "Bitcoin: A Peer-to-Peer Electronic Cash System,"[1] this seminal white paper delineated the tenets of a revolutionary digital currency that could be transmitted and received by users sans the necessity of a central governing body or financial institution acting as an intermediary. The white paper proposed the tantalizing concept of a purely peer-to-peer version of electronic cash that would allow online payments to be sent directly from one party to another without traversing through a financial institution.

The pivotal innovation underpinning Bitcoin was the distributed ledger recognized as the blockchain, a decentralized repository that securely and transparently logs every transaction in an immutable chain using cryptographic techniques. This groundbreaking technology eliminated the historical obstacle of double-spending that had long impeded the realization of digital currency.

The maiden Bitcoin transaction transpired on January 12, 2009, when Satoshi Nakamoto dispatched ten bitcoins to Hal Finney, a distinguished computer programmer, cypherpunk, and early proponent of Bitcoin. The inaugural block of the Bitcoin blockchain christened the Genesis block [2], was mined a few days later, on January 3, 2009, by Satoshi Nakamoto.

In its nascent stages, Bitcoin predominantly engaged a small cohort of developers, cryptographers, and enthusiasts captivated by its technological potential and the revolutionary concept of a decentralized digital currency beyond the control of governments or financial institutions. The primary Bitcoin exchange, Bitcoin Market [3], debuted in February 2010, facilitated by Dwdollar, and by May of the same year, the value of one bitcoin had surged to 1,000 bitcoins per US dollar.

As Bitcoin garnered momentum and global attention, more individuals gravitated towards mining and trading this trailblazing digital currency. In 2010, an event of historical significance unfolded as Laszlo Hanyecz, a programmer in Florida, expended 10,000 bitcoins for two Papa John's pizzas in what is considered the first real-world transaction involving bitcoin. This occurrence, commemorated annually as "Bitcoin Pizza Day"[4] on May 22nd, has become a cherished tradition within the cryptocurrency community, celebrating the humble beginnings of Bitcoin's journey towards mainstream adoption.

Over the ensuing years, Bitcoin's prominence swelled exponentially, with a proliferation of exchanges, businesses, and merchants embracing digital currency as a bona fide mode of transaction and store of value. However, Bitcoin's initial years were marked by trials, setbacks, and reversals. In 2011, the foremost Bitcoin exchange of the era, Mt. Gox [5], endured a substantial breach that led to the pilfering of thousands of bitcoins, foreshadowing the security vulnerabilities that would continue to plague the fledgling cryptocurrency ecosystem.

Despite these adversities and growing pains, Bitcoin persisted in gathering momentum, garnering a global following that embraced digital currency as both a revolutionary method of payment and an avenue for investment and wealth preservation beyond the purview of centralized authorities. Presently, Bitcoin reigns as the most prevalent and extensively utilized cryptocurrency, boasting a market capitalization surpassing $1 trillion as of 2021 and emerging as a formidable asset class that has captured the attention of institutional investors and financial heavyweights.

The ensuing chapter will delve into the early adopters, visionaries, and trailblazers of Bitcoin, elucidating their pivotal roles in shaping the embryonic advancement and expansion of this digital currency, as well as the challenges and controversies that threatened to derail its meteoric ascent.

1. https://bitcoin.org/en/bitcoin-paper
2. https://academy.binance.com/en/glossary/genesis-block
3. https://www.guinnessworldrecords.com/world-records/696258-first-cryptocurrency-exchange
4. https://nationaltoday.com/bitcoin-pizza-day/
5. https://www.investopedia.com/terms/m/mt-gox.asp

Chapter 2

Early Adopters and Pioneers

Bitcoin, that revolutionary digital currency, made its grand entrance onto the global stage courtesy of the enigmatic Satoshi Nakamoto in 2008. Nakamoto's seminal whitepaper, "Bitcoin: A Peer-to-Peer Electronic Cash System," laid a visionary blueprint for a decentralized digital currency that would function sans intermediaries such as banks or governments. This innovative concept held the tantalizing promise of democratizing the financial landscape and wresting control from the grip of centralized entities.

In the nascent days of Bitcoin, this digital marvel was primarily embraced by a small coterie of enthusiasts and tech lovers who recognized the seismic potential of this nascent technology. These pioneers were drawn in by Bitcoin's tantalizing promise of financial emancipation and a cloak of privacy, coupled with its capacity to disrupt the age-old edifice of conventional economic paradigms. They were the vanguards, unfurling a brave new world where transactions could transpire unfettered by the shackles of bureaucracy and government oversight.

Among the vanguard of Bitcoin's early disciples stands Gavin Andresen [1], a luminary figure in the digital currency landscape. Andresen, a virtuoso software developer, played an instrumental role in the formative years of Bitcoin, toiling in close quarters with the elusive Satoshi Nakamoto to refine and enhance the digital currency's underlying software architecture. His contributions were pivotal in shaping Bitcoin's evolution from a mere concept to a tangible, functional reality. Additionally, Andresen laid the cornerstone of the Bitcoin Foundation [2], an entity steadfast in its dedication to nurturing and fortifying the Bitcoin ecosystem, fostering its growth, and disseminating its ethos to a wider audience.

Another luminary figure in the annals of early Bitcoin adoption is Roger Ver [3], affectionately known as "Bitcoin Jesus." Ver emerged as a fervent evangelist for Bitcoin during its fledgling phase, leveraging his financial acumen to seed many Bitcoin startups and ventures. His unwavering conviction in the digital currency's transformative potential and his willingness to invest substantial resources into its burgeoning ecosystem played a crucial role in propelling Bitcoin's momentum. Notorious for his provocative stance on governance and regulation, Ver championed an ethos of decentralization and an unshackled financial landscape [4], where individuals could reclaim their fiscal autonomy.

Further luminaries in the pantheon of early Bitcoin champions include Charlie Shrem [5], a co-founder of the pioneering Bitcoin exchange BitInstant, and Nick Szabo, a luminary computer scientist widely attributed with a pivotal role in the genesis of Bitcoin's precursor, Bit Gold. Shrem's BitInstant stood as a beacon of hope for those seeking to traverse the uncharted territory of digital currency exchanges, while Szabo's visionary concepts [6] laid the conceptual foundation upon which Bitcoin would later be constructed.

As Bitcoin's momentum gathered relentlessly, a growing cohort of businesses and individuals [7] began to fathom the boundless potential of this digital currency. Entrepreneurs and innovators, endowed with an appetite for risk and a penchant for disruption, flocked to the Bitcoin arena, establishing exchanges, wallets, and other ancillary services to cater to the burgeoning demand. Simultaneously, a cadre of early investors, emboldened by Bitcoin's soaring valuation and the promise of astronomical returns, plunged headlong into this novel investment landscape.

The ensuing chapter will unravel the narrative of Bitcoin's ascent to the echelons of a mainstream payment medium and investment instrument while simultaneously exploring the crucible of challenges and opportunities that early adopters and investors confronted. It will delve into the trials and tribulations that marked this pioneering phase, shedding light on the regulatory hurdles, security breaches, and volatile price swings that threatened to derail Bitcoin's meteoric rise. Yet, through it all, the indomitable spirit of the early proponents shone through, steering Bitcoin towards unprecedented heights of acceptance and legitimacy.

1. http://gavinandresen.ninja/

2. https://www.bitcoinfoundation.org/
3. https://www.rogerver.com/
4. https://blockworks.co/news/roger-ver-right-bitcoin-book
5. https://www.charlieshrem.com/
6. https://www.brickken.com/en/post/blog-nick-szabo
7. https://www.cointree.com/learn/bitcoin-success-stories/

Chapter 3

The Emergence of Bitcoin Mining: From CPU to ASIC

In the grand tapestry of the Bitcoin network, one of its most pivotal facets lies in its decentralized architecture. This open framework extends an invitation to all, beckoning them to partake in the sacred duty of transaction verification and upholding the blockchain's sanctity. This holy ritual, aptly named mining, entails the artful deployment of computational prowess to unravel formidable mathematical enigmas, reaping the rewards of freshly minted bitcoins.

In the genesis days of Bitcoin, mining was a relatively straightforward affair, amenable to execution through a run-of-the-mill computer's CPU. The fledgling miners, a devoted cadre of cypherpunks and technophiles, wielded their desktop machines as virtual pickaxes [1], chipping away at the blockchain's byzantine puzzles with unbridled fervor.

Yet, as the network burgeoned and a phalanx of miners rallied to the cause, the bar was raised. The mining terrain morphed into an arena necessitating augmented computational might and specialized hardware to hold one's own.

The epochal shift in Bitcoin mining annals transpired in 2010, bearing the moniker of GPU mining. Graphics Processing Units (GPUs), erstwhile architects of virtual worlds in video games, unfurled their latent potential for Bitcoin mining. Their parallel processing prowess bestowed upon them an edge, rendering them akin to a cadre of industrious workers toiling in unison to outpace their CPU predecessors. GPU mining [2] swiftly ascended to the throne as the favored modus operandi for myriad miners, heralding a quantum leap in mining efficiency vis-à-vis CPU mining.

Nonetheless, GPU mining's reign was brief, eclipsed by the advent of a specialized breed of hardware called Application-Specific Integrated Circuits, or ASICs. These marvels are meticulously crafted for the singular purpose of mining bitcoins, endowing practitioners with a quantum leap in mining efficiency and velocity compared to their GPU forebears. Akin to a phalanx of finely-tuned centurions, ASICs marshaled their computational might, rendering their predecessors obsolete in the hallowed quest for bitcoin riches. In today's milieu, ASICs reign supreme in Bitcoin mining [3], rendering it a Sisyphean endeavor for individual miners to vie with behemoth mining conglomerates wielding formidable computational artillery.

The advent of ASICs reverberated across the Bitcoin landscape with profound repercussions. On one flank, it ushered in a centralization of mining clout within the bastions of a select few, a development some posit as an existential threat to the network's decentralization ethos. The once egalitarian mining landscape, where any soul could join the fray armed with a modest computer, had metamorphosed into an arena dominated by industrial-scale mining operations undergirded by prodigious capital and cutting-edge hardware.

Conversely, ASICs' arrival fortified the ramparts of the web, rendering it a more impregnable fortress against marauding malefactors seeking to usurp the network or orchestrate 51% of attacks. The sheer computational [4] might marshaled by these specialized mining rigs acts as a bulwark, rendering nefarious efforts to subvert the blockchain a herculean, if not quixotic, endeavor.

Despite ASICs' stranglehold on Bitcoin mining [5,] there persists an ardor to democratize the process for the individual miner. One such endeavor lies in the crucible of crafting mining hardware with a penchant for myriad cryptocurrencies, affording miners the liberty to flit between coins contingent on the caprices of the market. By diversifying their mining portfolios, these intrepid souls could hedge against the volatility of any single cryptocurrency while leveraging their hardware investments across a spectrum of digital assets.

Additionally, concerted efforts are underway to usher in an era of sustainable and energy-efficient mining, leveraging renewable energy sources and refining the efficacy of mining hardware. As the environmental ramifications of mining have come under scrutiny, a vanguard of innovators has arisen, striving to strike a harmonious balance between the insatiable demand for computational power and the exigencies of ecological stewardship. From harnessing the latent potential of hydroelectric, solar, and wind energy to optimizing the thermal dynamics of mining rigs, these endeavors seek to forge a greener path for Bitcoin mining [6].

All in all, the saga of Bitcoin mining, from its humble origins in CPU mining to the ascendance of specialized ASICs, constitutes a riveting and integral chapter in the annals of Bitcoin lore. As the network continues its relentless march, the evolution of mining technology and methodologies promises to be a chronicle well worth watching. Whether it be the emergence of new hardware paradigms, innovative energy solutions, or novel approaches to decentralization, the realm of Bitcoin mining stands poised to script an enthralling narrative in the years to come.

1. https://www.quora.com/How-did-people-mine-Bitcoins-back-in-2009-Was-it-by-solving-code-problems-or-just-by-simply-logging-into-a-website
2. https://pontem.network/posts/the-evolution-of-bitcoin-mining
3. https://coinmarketcap.com/academy/article/what-is-asic-mining
4. https://www.coindesk.com/tech/2020/04/26/the-rise-of-asics-a-step-by-step-history-of-bitcoin-mining/

5. https://www.linkedin.com/pulse/detailed-analysis-asic-bitcoin-mining-hardware-market/
6. https://compassmining.io/education/green-bitcoin-mining-harnessing-methane-from-animal-waste-for-a-sustainable-crypto-future/

Chapter 4

Bitcoin Goes Mainstream: Its Rise to Prominence

In the nascent days of Bitcoin, a close-knit cadre of impassioned enthusiasts were captivated by the tantalizing promise of decentralization and emancipation from the clutches of conventional financial monoliths. These ardent proponents, hailing from the fringes of the internet's crevasses and dimly-lit hacker enclaves, prophesied a future where the immutable laws of mathematics would dethrone the ivory towers of centralized authority, unfurling an era of unparalleled financial autonomy.

However, as the sands of time trickled by, Bitcoin's siren call began to resonate far beyond the realm of these early evangelists, beckoning mainstream investors, visionary entrepreneurs, and discerning businesses into its fold. What was once a niche fascination confined to the fringes had blossomed into a phenomenon that could no longer be ignored.

A pivotal catalyst in Bitcoin's ascent to the echelons of prominence was the crescendo of media attention it garnered. In 2013, they witnessed a watershed moment as Bitcoin graced the hallowed front page of The New York Times [1], a move that kindled an inferno of intrigue and speculation. This seminal event was merely the prelude [2], as a cavalcade of media spotlights and resounding endorsements from luminaries and moguls amplified Bitcoin's resonance among the masses, thrusting it into the zeitgeist of popular culture.

With burgeoning popularity, a sea change unfurled as businesses commenced accepting Bitcoin as payment. 2014 saw industry stalwarts like Microsoft [3], Expedia, and Overstock.com embracing Bitcoin for their wares and services, a clarion call heralding a paradigm shift in corporate attitudes towards cryptocurrency. This trend burgeoned in subsequent years, with a burgeoning cadre of merchants and retailers extending open arms to Bitcoin and an array of fellow cryptocurrencies, emboldened by the promise of frictionless global transactions and newfound financial flexibility.

Yet another fulcrum in Bitcoin's ascendancy was the burgeoning interest from institutional titans, entities that had erstwhile dismissed the phenomenon as a fleeting fad. In 2017, the Chicago Mercantile Exchange [4] and the

Chicago Board Options Exchange [5] unfurled the canvas of Bitcoin futures contracts, a watershed moment empowering institutional behemoths to stake their claims on the future trajectory of Bitcoin's value. This clarion call was echoed by various financial juggernauts, including Goldman Sachs and JPMorgan, who embarked on quests to assimilate Bitcoin into their hallowed investment strategies, recognizing the technology's disruptive potential.

Simultaneously, the crucible of Bitcoin's rise bore witness to the genesis of a vibrant and dynamic community of developers, entrepreneurs, and enthusiasts. This fraternity played a pivotal role in propelling the Bitcoin ecosystem into an era of unprecedented growth and innovation, birthing fresh applications and vistas for the technology, and shattering preconceived notions of the boundaries of decentralized digital currencies. Visionaries and tinkerers alike endeavored to harness the transformative potential of blockchain technology, with their ingenuity birthing a cornucopia of newfangled applications and services that threatened to upend traditional paradigms.

Yet, this meteoric rise has not been without its crucibles. The cryptocurrency realm grappled with a litany of regulatory stumbling blocks and security breaches, with high-profile hacks and heists etching themselves into the annals of Bitcoin lore. The decentralized nature that was once heralded as a panacea for financial autonomy became a double-edged sword, as bad actors exploited vulnerabilities in the ecosystem, absconding with millions in digital assets and sowing seeds of mistrust.

Furthermore, the mercurial price trajectory of Bitcoin has thrust it into the crucible of intense speculation and vigorous debate, with dissenting voices prophesying a bubble poised for rupture. The stratospheric valuations witnessed in the cryptocurrency's ascent have been punctuated by precipitous plunges, igniting a polarizing discourse on the true nature and sustainability of this nascent asset class.

Despite these tribulations, the resounding prominence of Bitcoin stands as a testament to its mettle. Its transformative influence on the broader financial tapestry is undeniable, catalyzing a paradigm shift in how we perceive and interact with money. As an ever-increasing cadre of businesses and institutions extend their embrace to Bitcoin and its kin, it is palpable that we are but skimming the surface of the boundless possibilities harbored within this revolutionary technology. The decentralized future that once seemed a distant fantasy is inexorably coalescing into reality, propelled by the indomitable spirit of innovation that has become inextricably intertwined with the Bitcoin ethos.

1. https://archive.nytimes.com/dealbook.nytimes.com/2013/11/27/a-prediction-bitcoin-is-doomed-to-fail/
2. https://www.vice.com/en/article/dypkbx/bitcoin-2013-conference-charlie-shrem-cryptoland
3. https://qrius.com/7-major-companies-that-accept-bitcoin-payments-in-2023/

4. https://www.cmegroup.com/media-room/press-releases/2017/12/01/cme_group_self-certifiesbitcoinfuturestolaunchdec18.html
5. https://www.cboe.com/

Chapter 5

The Technology Behind Bitcoin

Nestled at the core of Bitcoin's seismic potential lies its foundational technology—the blockchain [1]. This decentralized digital ledger, anointed with the name "blockchain," stands as a sentinel, dutifully chronicling transactions with a blend of security and transparency, unfettered by intermediaries such as banks or financial institutions. It is a revolutionary technology that has captured the imagination of visionaries and disruptors alike, heralding a paradigm shift in how we perceive and facilitate transactions.

Shepherding this digital realm is a cadre of custodians known as nodes. These sentinels, scattered across the globe, undertake the solemn charge of verifying and sanctifying transactions that traverse the web. Each transaction finds its eternal abode within a block and, from thenceforth, becomes an indelible and immutable part of the chain of blocks, forever etching its mark on the annals of the network. This unerring process bequeaths an immutable testament to the integrity and transparency of the system, a stark contrast to the opaque and often inscrutable machinations of traditional financial systems.

Yet, the pièce de résistance of the blockchain lies in its imperviousness to tampering or subversion. Each block in this hallowed chain boasts a unique cryptographic signature [2], thwarting any audacious attempts to meddle with its sanctity. This cryptographic fortification, forged through the alchemical fusion of advanced mathematics and computer science, renders the blockchain virtually impervious to malicious actors or nefarious forces seeking to corrupt the system. Any endeavor to alter the chain is swiftly and decisively rebuffed by the vigilant nodes safeguarding the network's sanctity. Thus, the blockchain is an impregnable fortress, a bastion of security for recording transactions, a beacon of trust in an increasingly distrustful digital landscape.

Complementing this tower is the crucible of Bitcoin mining, which bestows miners the mantle of guardianship over the network. In exchange for their computational prowess, miners are rewarded with freshly minted Bitcoin—digital tokens that hold immense value and promise in the burgeoning world of cryptocurrencies. Armed with specialized technology and software, these miners embark on the arduous task of solving intricate mathematical conundrums—puzzles that serve as the gatekeepers for new blocks seeking entry into the blockchain's hallowed ranks.

The mining process, deliberately designed to be an uphill battle, serves as a bulwark against any single entity amassing undue influence over the network. It is a decentralized endeavor, where miners from across the globe contribute their computational might, ensuring that no single individual or organization holds sway over the system. With the arrival of new miners, the puzzles evolve into even more formidable challenges, demanding a surge in computational might to surmount. This ever-escalating difficulty[3] ensures that the network remains secure, resilient, and decentralized, while simultaneously bestowing rewards upon those who contribute to its upkeep.

This process bears the hallmark of a finite supply, with a predetermined 21 million Bitcoin[4] slated to exist. As the Bitcoin trove is gradually unearthed, the spoils for each block dwindle, posing an escalating challenge for miners to amass significant rewards. This scarcity, coupled with the ever-increasing demand for Bitcoin, has fueled its meteoric rise in value, captivating investors and speculators alike.

In summation, the technological scaffolding underpinning Bitcoin stands as a linchpin in its trajectory, a testament to the ingenuity and foresight of its creators. The blockchain, a paragon of decentralization, transparency, and security, presides over this digital realm, ushering in a new era of trust and accountability in transactions. Simultaneously, the crucible of mining stands sentinel, safeguarding the network's integrity and apportioning Bitcoin judiciously among its stewards. It is a delicate balance, a symphony of computational power and cryptographic elegance, forging a path towards a future where traditional financial intermediaries may become obsolete, replaced by a decentralized, trustless system that empowers individuals and challenges the status quo.

In the forthcoming chapter, we shall embark on a voyage delving into the potential applications of blockchain technology, a force poised to revolutionize a manifold array of industries. From supply chain management to voting systems, from real estate transactions to intellectual property rights, the blockchain's disruptive potential knows no bounds. We shall explore how this disruptive technology might reshape the very fabric of our society, ushering in a new era of transparency, accountability, and trust in the digital age.

1. https://www.pwc.com/us/en/industries/financial-services/fintech/bitcoin-blockchain-cryptocurrency.html
2. https://www.pwc.com/us/en/industries/financial-services/fintech/bitcoin-blockchain-cryptocurrency.html
3. https://www.coinwarz.com/mining/bitcoin/difficulty-chart
4. https://river.com/learn/what-will-happen-after-all-bitcoin-mined/

Chapter 6

The Future of Blockchain Technology

While Bitcoin is the vanguard of blockchain technology, its prowess extends far beyond digital currencies. The decentralized and transparent ethos that defines blockchain can potentially transmute a panoply of industries, ranging from finance and real estate to healthcare and supply chain management.

In the realm of finance, blockchain's foray promises a paradigm shift. It could pave the way for seamless and cost-effective cross-border money transfers, concurrently mitigating fraud and money laundering. By eliminating the need for intermediaries, blockchain could usher in an era of reduced transaction costs and enhanced efficiency [1]. Moreover, the technology bears the promise of birthing novel financial instruments, giving rise to decentralized lending platforms and peer-to-peer insurance networks. These decentralized platforms could democratize access to financial services, empowering individuals and communities that have traditionally been underserved by traditional financial institutions.

The real estate sector, too, stands poised for transformation. Blockchain's advent could unfurl a tapestry of streamlined and secure property transactions, augmenting the sanctity of property titles and associated documents. By maintaining an immutable and transparent record of property ownership [2], blockchain could mitigate disputes and expedite the transfer of real estate assets. This could usher in an era of reduced fraudulence and heightened transparency within the real estate sphere, engendering trust and confidence among buyers, sellers, and intermediaries alike.

The healthcare arena, often bedeviled by data security concerns, is another bastion awaiting blockchain's transformative touch. By bestowing upon us secure and decentralized repositories for medical data, patients could assert greater dominion over their health information. This could empower individuals to selectively share their medical records with healthcare providers, fostering a more collaborative and patient-centric approach to healthcare delivery. Simultaneously, it would simplify the task for healthcare providers to access and disseminate medical records [3], ushering in an era of streamlined healthcare delivery, while ensuring data integrity and patient privacy.

The supply chain realm, often grappling with issues of authenticity and traceability, emerges as another crucible for blockchain's potential. The technology's transparent and secure ledger systems could serve as sentinels, diligently tracking goods and vouchsafing their authenticity. By creating an immutable record of a product's journey from origin to destination [4], blockchain could unveil unprecedented levels of transparency, enabling consumers to make informed decisions and holding companies accountable for their supply chain practices. This, in turn, could herald a renaissance, curtailing the scourge of fraud and counterfeiting and enhancing the overall efficacy of supply chain operations.

Beyond these realms, blockchain's disruptive potential extends to domains such as voting systems, digital identity management, and intellectual property rights. By leveraging the technology's inherent attributes of decentralization, transparency, and immutability, we could forge more secure and trustworthy systems for democratic processes, identity verification, and the protection of creative works.

Though blockchain technology is nascent, its potential applications are as boundless as their horizons. As industries embark on journeys of exploration, we stand poised to witness a symphony of novel and ingenious applications unfold in the years ahead. However, this transformative journey is not without its challenges. Issues such as scalability, energy consumption, and regulatory uncertainty must be addressed to pave the way for widespread adoption. Nonetheless, the promise of blockchain technology looms large, beckoning us to embrace a future where trust, transparency, and decentralization are the bedrock of our digital ecosystems.

1. https://www2.deloitte.com/us/en/pages/consulting/articles/future-of-blockchain.html

2. https://www.financemagnates.com/cryptocurrency/education-centre/the-impact-of-cryptocurrency-on-the-real-estate-industry/
3. https://www.webmd.com/a-to-z-guides/features/blockchain-healthcare
4. https://hbr.org/2020/05/building-a-transparent-supply-chain

Chapter 7

Challenges and Criticisms of Bitcoin

Despite Bitcoin's meteoric rise to fame and acceptance since its inception, it has encountered numerous formidable challenges and criticisms. In this chapter, we shall embark on a journey to unearth some of the most poignant issues confronting Bitcoin and the expansive cryptocurrency landscape.

Foremost among these challenges is the erratic nature of Bitcoin's value. Its market price has been a turbulent sea, known to churn and surge with wild abandon. Price fluctuations [1] of seismic proportions unfurl in hours, even minutes. This capriciousness poses a daunting hurdle for consumers and businesses, casting a shadow on Bitcoin's utility as a stable store of value or a dependable medium of exchange. The volatility stems, in part, from the relatively shallow liquidity pool and the speculative fervor that surrounds the cryptocurrency market. As institutional investors and regulatory frameworks gradually take root, there is hope that such turbulence may subside, ushering in an era of greater price stability.

Another thorn in Bitcoin's side is its potential for nefarious exploits [2]. The cloak of anonymity and decentralization that enshrouds Bitcoin transactions has been leveraged for sinister ends, becoming an unwitting accomplice to money laundering, drug trafficking, and other illicit activities. While concerted efforts are underway to fortify transparency and curtail avenues for unlawful exploitation, this specter continues to loom large in the eyes of policymakers and regulators. Initiatives such as Know Your Customer [3] (KYC) and Anti-Money Laundering [4] (AML) protocols aim to strike a delicate balance between preserving user privacy and mitigating the risk of criminal misuse.

A litany of reproaches also surrounds Bitcoin's voracious appetite for energy. The mining process, a crucible for forging new blocks into the blockchain, exacts a prodigious toll on resources, demanding staggering amounts of computational might and electricity. This voracity has ignited apprehensions about Bitcoin's environmental footprint, casting a pall over its sustainability and triggering reflections on its effects on the global ecosystem. Proponents argue that the energy consumption is justified by the creation of a robust, decentralized financial system, while detractors contend that the costs outweigh the benefits. As the clamor for eco-friendly solutions intensifies, the onus falls on the cryptocurrency community to explore avenues for mitigating this energy burden, be it through more efficient mining hardware, renewable energy sources, or alternative consensus mechanisms.

Finally, there looms the specter of scalability, an issue that reverberates through the corridors of Bitcoin's infrastructure. As the ranks of users swell and transactions surge, there exists a palpable risk of the system succumbing to congestion, culminating in protracted transaction times and inflated fees. While valiant strides are being taken to redress this concern, it remains an imposing bastion for the cryptocurrency realm. Proposed solutions, such as the Lightning Network [5] and sharding [6], aim to alleviate the strain on the blockchain by facilitating off-chain transactions and partitioning the network, respectively. However, their adoption and efficacy remain subject to ongoing debate and scrutiny.

Yet, amidst these crucibles, Bitcoin and its ilk persist, evolving and expanding. As the tapestry of technology continues to weave, solutions will invariably emerge to grapple with these challenges. However, it behooves us to remain vigilant, addressing nascent risks and concerns as they surface to safeguard the enduring prosperity and expansion of the cryptocurrency domain. Collaboration between industry stakeholders, policymakers, and the broader public is paramount to strike a harmonious chord between innovation and responsible stewardship.

In the chapters that follow, we shall delve deeper into these issues, dissecting their nuances and exploring the myriad proposals and initiatives aimed at resolving them. For Bitcoin to truly realize its potential as a disruptive force in the financial realm, these challenges must be confronted head-on, with unwavering determination and a spirit of collective ingenuity.

1. https://www.statista.com/statistics/326707/bitcoin-price-index/
2. https://www.cvedetails.com/vulnerability-list/vendor_id-12094/Bitcoin.html
3. https://crypto.com/university/what-is-kyc-in-crypto
4. https://www.elliptic.co/anti-money-laundering-aml-in-cryptocurrency
5. https://lightning.network/
6. https://www.coinbase.com/learn/advanced-trading/what-is-crypto-sharding-and-how-does-it-work

Chapter 8

Regulatory Landscape for Bitcoin

The regulatory milieu governing cryptocurrency and Bitcoin is a dynamic tapestry subject to constant flux and evolution. Countries have approached this nascent industry with a diverse array of strategies, ranging from open-armed embrace to guarded reservation and even outright hostility. In this chapter, we embark on a journey through the various approaches adopted by nations in regulating Bitcoin.

In the United States, Bitcoin is classified as a commodity, falling under the purview of the Commodity Futures Trading Commission [1] (CFTC). In tandem, the Securities and Exchange Commission [2] (SEC) has taken a stand against fraudulent Initial Coin Offerings [3] (ICOs). Nevertheless, the SEC has yet to furnish explicit directives on the future regulation of cryptocurrencies. This regulatory ambiguity has generated uncertainty within the industry, prompting calls for a more comprehensive framework to be established.

Japan, on the other hand, has extended a warm embrace to Bitcoin, recognizing it as a bona fide form of payment since 2016 [4]. The nation has fostered a relatively pleasant environment for the industry to thrive, enacting legislation to govern cryptocurrency exchanges and implementing measures to curb money laundering and terrorist financing. This regulatory clarity has ushered in a wave of institutional adoption, with major financial institutions and corporations delving into the cryptocurrency sphere.

In stark contrast, China has unfurled a more adversarial banner, casting a shadow on the cryptocurrency landscape. The country has imposed stringent measures, including prohibiting Initial Coin Offerings (ICOs) and a crackdown on cryptocurrency exchanges. This hardline stance has stemmed from concerns over financial stability, capital outflows, and the potential for cryptocurrencies to be exploited for nefarious purposes. Nonetheless, China's approach has not entirely extinguished the cryptocurrency flame within its borders [5], as mining operations and peer-to-peer trading continue to persist, albeit in murkier waters.

Across Europe, the regulatory landscape splinters into a mosaic of approaches. Nations like Malta have extended a friendly hand to the industry [6], enacting legislation to establish a comprehensive regulatory framework and positioning themselves as a hub for blockchain and cryptocurrency businesses. Conversely, others like Germany have adopted a more cautious stance [7], subjecting cryptocurrency transactions to stringent anti-money laundering and counter-terrorism financing regulations.

At a supra-national level, the European Union has wielded its influence [8], enacting new provisions targeting anti-money laundering and counter-terrorism financing, slated to take effect in 2021. These regulations mandate that cryptocurrency exchanges and custodial wallet providers comply with stringent Know Your Customer (KYC) and Anti-Money Laundering (AML) protocols, further emphasizing the need for transparency and accountability within the industry.

In Africa, the regulatory arena [9] is marked by a relative need for more formal frameworks governing the cryptocurrency sphere. However, strides have been made in countries such as Nigeria and South Africa as they take nascent steps towards formulating regulations. Nigeria has unveiled plans to develop a comprehensive regulatory framework for cryptocurrencies, while South Africa has established a regulatory working group to explore potential guidelines.

As a collective whole, the regulatory landscape governing cryptocurrency and Bitcoin is a labyrinthine expanse, forever in flux. With the industry hurtling towards growth and maturation, one can anticipate the emergence of fresh regulations and guidelines on a global scale. These regulations will likely seek to strike a balance between fostering innovation and mitigating risks associated with cryptocurrencies, such as financial instability, money laundering, and terrorist financing.

It will be incumbent upon businesses and investors entrenched in the cryptocurrency domain to remain vigilant, stay abreast of the latest regulatory developments, and adhere to pertinent laws and regulations to sidestep legal or financial entanglements. Compliance measures, such as robust KYC and AML protocols, will become increasingly pivotal as the industry navigates the ever-evolving regulatory terrain.

Furthermore, the industry must engage in proactive dialogue with regulatory bodies, advocating for clear and sensible regulations that facilitate innovation while safeguarding consumer interests and upholding financial integrity. Collaboration between industry stakeholders and regulators will be crucial in shaping a regulatory framework that nurtures the growth of cryptocurrencies while mitigating potential risks.

As the cryptocurrency ecosystem continues to expand and permeate mainstream finance, the regulatory landscape will undoubtedly undergo seismic shifts, with nations continuously re-evaluating and refining their approaches. It is a journey fraught with challenges and opportunities, one that will shape the future trajectory of this burgeoning technological revolution.

1. https://www.cftc.gov/
2. https://www.sec.gov/
3. https://www.europarl.europa.eu/RegData/etudes/BRIE/2021/696167/EPRS_BRI(2021)696167_EN.pdf
4. https://www.sygna.io/blog/japan-crypto-regulation-history-2014-2020/

5. https://www.reuters.com/technology/bruised-by-stock-market-chinese-rush-into-banned-bitcoin-2024-01-25/
6. https://www.forbes.com/sites/rachelwolfson/2018/07/05/maltese-parliament-passes-laws-that-set-regulatory-framework-for-blockchain-cryptocurrency-and-dlt/
7. https://www.cnbc.com/id/100971898
8. https://finance.ec.europa.eu/digital-finance/crypto-assets_en
9. https://www.economist.com/middle-east-and-africa/2024/03/07/why-africa-is-cryptos-next-frontier

Chapter 9

Bitcoin's Competitors: The Rise of Alternative Cryptocurrencies

Bitcoin, often hailed as the sovereign of cryptocurrencies reigns supreme, but it stands far from solitary in its dominion. Over time, a phalanx of alternative cryptocurrencies, christened "altcoins," have risen, each bearing its distinct attributes and value proposition, posing an intriguing inquiry – could their ascendance impinge upon Bitcoin's throne?

Among the earliest progeny of Bitcoin stands Litecoin [1], a luminary in the pantheon of alternative cryptocurrencies. Forged in the crucible of 2011, Litecoin's ambition was clear: to birth a nimbler and lighter counterpart to Bitcoin. Diverging with its unique mining algorithm [2] and abbreviated block generation time, it bestows the gift of swifter transaction processing. However, some detractors contend that Litecoin's deviations from Bitcoin's script render it a mere auxiliary, bereft of the audacity to supplant its progenitor.

Ethereum [3], a luminary in its own right, deviates from the trajectory of Bitcoin and Litecoin. It is a sprawling platform, a fertile ground where visionaries can breathe life into smart contracts and decentralized applications. Furthermore, it unfurls a canvas for crafting custom tokens, sowing the seeds for a burgeoning crop of nascent cryptocurrencies. With its versatility and malleability, Ethereum poses a formidable challenge to Bitcoin's predominance [4], as it transcends the scope of a mere currency to become a canvas for innovation.

Ripple [5], with its gaze firmly fixed on the horizon, endeavors to streamline cross-border payments, a realm where Bitcoin's cumbersome protocols render it ill-suited. By harnessing a centralized ledger, Ripple promises to expedite transactions and foster seamless international fund transfers. Its partnerships with established financial institutions lend it a legitimacy that few altcoins can boast, casting doubts upon Bitcoin's capacity to reign supreme in the realm of global finance.

Bitcoin Cash [6], an offshoot of the original Bitcoin network, bears the standard of reduced fees and accelerated transaction times. Its proponents espouse it as a purer embodiment of Satoshi Nakamoto's vision, unfettered by the shackles of congestion and exorbitant costs that have plagued Bitcoin's ascent. With its larger block sizes and a growing community of adherents, Bitcoin Cash poses a direct challenge [7] to its predecessor's hegemony.

Tether, in a league of its own, stands as a stablecoin, tethered to the sanctity of the U.S. dollar. Its allure lies in its capacity to mitigate the volatility that plagues conventional cryptocurrencies, rendering it a haven for those seeking a bridge between the fiat and digital realms. While it may lack the ambition to dethrone Bitcoin, its utility as a medium of exchange and store of value cannot be discounted.

While Bitcoin retains its scepter as the pinnacle of cryptocurrencies, the emergence of alternatives begets profound questions regarding its enduring supremacy. Could the rise of these contenders pose an existential threat to Bitcoin's hegemony in the cryptocurrency realm? Some contend that Bitcoin's pioneering role and widespread adoption cement its position as the lodestar of long-term success. Others assert that the alternatives' capacity to address Bitcoin's shortcomings and adapt to evolving market demands render them formidable adversaries.

In the grand tapestry of destiny, myriad variables shall shape the fates of Bitcoin and its brethren. Their capacity to scale, the regulatory firmament they navigate, and their efficacy in addressing critical use cases and meeting the difficulties of their users shall all figure into the equation. The ongoing debates surrounding decentralization, privacy, and scalability shall undoubtedly influence the trajectory of these digital assets.

As the landscape of cryptocurrency continues its inexorable metamorphosis, witnessing the evolution of Bitcoin and the trajectory of its challengers promises to be a narrative of intrigue and fascination in the years to unfold. Will Bitcoin's first-mover advantage and brand recognition prove an impregnable bastion? Or will the agility and innovation of the altcoins gradually erode its dominance, ushering in a new era of decentralized finance? Only time shall unveil the denouement of this captivating saga.

1. https://litecoin.org/
2. https://elementalcrypto.com/tips-and-tricks/litecoin-mining-algorithm/
3. https://ethereum.org/en/
4. https://crypto.com/bitcoin/bitcoin-vs-ethereum-whats-the-difference-between-btc-and-eth
5. https://ripple.com/
6. https://bitcoincash.org/
7. https://www.fool.com/terms/b/bitcoin-cash/

Chapter 10

Future of Bitcoin

The impact of Bitcoin and its cryptocurrency brethren on technology and finance is already large, but what destiny awaits this industry? In this chapter, we shall peer into the crystal ball, discerning the formidable trends and innovations poised to sculpt the future of Bitcoin and its ilk.

Foremost among these nascent trends is the surging adoption of blockchain technology by enterprises and governments [1]. This formidable juggernaut can potentially transmute myriad industries, from supply chain orchestration to the very bedrock of democratic societies - voting systems. As corporations and governments dip their toes into blockchain experimentation, the clamor for cryptocurrencies is poised to crescendo.

Enterprises are enticed by the immutable and transparent nature of blockchain ledgers, which could instill newfound efficiencies in supply chains by providing an unassailable record of product provenance and movement. Furthermore, blockchain-based smart contracts could automate and streamline manifold business processes. Governmental interests, on the other hand, are piqued by the potentially transformative application of blockchain for secure digital voting that could bolster democracy's integrity.

Another luminary in the constellation of trends is the ascendant role of stablecoins [2]. These digital currencies, tethered to the value of tangible assets like the U.S. dollar or even the age-old allure of gold, stand resolute against the turbulent tides of volatility that buffet their cryptocurrency kin. This stability renders them an alluring prospect for businesses and consumers, serving as a medium of exchange or a bastion for storing value.

The ascent of stablecoins could be propelled by their utility as gateways into the cryptocurrency ecosystem for institutions wary of the volatility intrinsic to pioneering digital assets like Bitcoin. Businesses could leverage stablecoins for secure and rapid transactions, circumventing the fees and delays endemic to traditional cross-border payments. Consumers too may gravitate towards stablecoins as mediums of exchange, affording the conveniences of cryptocurrencies without the recurrent risk of dramatic value fluctuations.

Simultaneously, the clarion call for cryptocurrencies as conduits for remittances and cross-border transactions resounds with increasing fervor. The conventional banking apparatus, though stalwart, often lacks the humility demanded when confronted with the swiftness and frugality required by international transactions. Here, cryptocurrencies emerge as potential avatars of rapidity, cost-efficiency, and fortified security in cross-border remittances.

The hamstrung efficiencies and opaque costs associated with traditional remittance channels could catalyze the widespread adoption of cryptocurrencies for international money transfers [3]. The pseudonymous nature of many cryptocurrencies, combined with their ability to transcend borders seamlessly, positions them as consummate solutions for remittances, particularly in regions with underdeveloped financial infrastructure or where capital controls stymie the flow of funds.

Last, but by no means least, emerges the burgeoning interest in the potential of Bitcoin and fellow cryptocurrencies as hedges against the specter of inflation and economic vicissitude. With the global economy navigating treacherous waters, the stormy seas of the COVID-19 pandemic, and geopolitical skirmishes, some investors are turning to cryptocurrencies as lifeboats to safeguard their financial moorings.

The immutable scarcity of Bitcoin, coupled with its lack of centralized oversight or control, has catalyzed viewpoints that it could serve as a bulwark against inflation driven by excessive money printing or erosion of faith in fiat currencies. Furthermore, the decentralized and borderless nature of cryptocurrencies could render them sanctuaries for capital preservation amidst economic turmoil or conflicts that disrupt traditional financial systems.

While the vista of Bitcoin and the cryptocurrency domain remains shrouded in a veil of uncertainty, one thing is abundantly clear. This industry is poised for an evolution of seismic proportions, destined to reshape the contours of finance and technology. As new frontiers of technology and utility unfurl, it becomes incumbent upon businesses and investors to remain vigilant, abreast of the latest developments, and poised to seize the opportunities presented by this rapidly burgeoning landscape.

The road ahead for Bitcoin and cryptocurrencies is fraught with challenges and obstacles. Regulatory uncertainties, technical limitations, and philosophical debates [4] over decentralization and governance loom large. However, the groundswell of interest and innovation permeating this sphere portends a future where digital assets could become integral components of the global financial fabric. As this domain matures and evolves, those who remain adaptable and forward-thinking may reap the windfall of opportunities that this audacious frontier of finance [5] has to offer.

1. https://www.gemini.com/cryptopedia/blockchain-governance-mechanisms
2. https://www.coindesk.com/business/2024/04/09/stablecoins-are-seeing-adoption-as-a-cross-border-settlement-mechanism-bernstein/

3. https://stormgain.com/blog/crypto-for-international-money-transfers
4. https://journals.sagepub.com/doi/10.1177/02632764211049826
5. https://www.cfr.org/backgrounder/crypto-question-bitcoin-digital-dollars-and-future-money

Chapter 11

Risks and Challenges of Bitcoin

While the allure of Bitcoin and its cryptocurrency kin is undeniable, they are not without their perils and pitfalls. In this chapter, we shall embark on an odyssey through the key risks and tribulations besetting the Bitcoin industry.

Foremost among these potential perils is the specter of volatility [1]. The value of Bitcoin is known to oscillate with the capriciousness of a storm, rendering it an unreliable bedrock for businesses and investors seeking stability in the seas of exchange and store of value. While the historical trajectory of Bitcoin's price has unfurled skyward, there exists no guarantor of this unbroken ascent. The cryptocurrency's value [2] is susceptible to the whims of market sentiment, news cycles, and external economic factors, prompting dramatic fluctuations that can upend financial plans and projections.

In the labyrinth of risks, the peril of hacking and theft looms large. Once a Bitcoin transaction is etched into the ledger, no recourse exists for the reclamation of pilfered or lost Bitcoins. The annals of cryptocurrency history bear witness to a litany of high-profile breaches and security lapses at exchanges and wallets, casting a pall of uncertainty over the security of the cryptocurrency ecosystem. The pseudonymous nature of Bitcoin transactions and the irreversibility of the blockchain further compound the challenges of recovering stolen funds, underscoring the need for robust security measures and due diligence in safeguarding digital assets.

The shadow of regulatory risk [3] darkens the horizon as well. While some governments embrace cryptocurrencies, others approach them with circumspection or hostility. Modifications in regulation bear the potential to shape the trajectory of cryptocurrency growth and adoption, prompting businesses and investors to remain vigilant to the potential regulatory entanglements associated with this technology. The lack of a unified global framework for cryptocurrency regulation engenders uncertainty, as jurisdictions grapple with the complexities of taxation, anti-money laundering measures, and the integration of digital assets into existing financial infrastructures.

Lastly, the risk is that Bitcoin and its brethren may fail to pursue mainstream adoption [4]. Though the cryptocurrency industry has burgeoned in recent years, it remains a relatively niche enclave compared to the well-entrenched edifice of traditional financial systems. For Bitcoin and its counterparts to claim the mantle of widespread adoption, they must surmount a gauntlet of technical, regulatory, and societal barriers. The complexities of blockchain technology, the perceived anonymity of transactions, and the lingering skepticism of established financial institutions all pose formidable obstacles to mainstream acceptance.

Furthermore, the environmental impact of Bitcoin's energy-intensive mining process has drawn scrutiny and criticism, potentially hindering its adoption by eco-conscious consumers and businesses. The decentralized nature of the Bitcoin network, while a strength in many regards, also presents challenges in terms of governance and consensus-building, as the lack of a central authority can impede coordinated efforts to address emergent issues or implement updates.

In summation, while the promise of Bitcoin and other cryptocurrencies is palpable, they bear risks and challenges. Businesses and investors must tread with circumspection, meticulously weighing these perils and tribulations before immersing themselves in cryptocurrencies. Remaining attuned to the latest advancements in this swiftly evolving landscape is imperative in navigating the intricate tapestry of risks accompanying this technology. As the cryptocurrency ecosystem matures, addressing these challenges will be crucial to realizing the transformative potential of this disruptive innovation.

1. https://www.vaneck.com/us/en/blogs/digital-assets/bitcoin-volatility/
2. https://portal.ct.gov/dob/consumer/consumer-education/cryptocurrency-risks
3. https://www.investopedia.com/terms/c/cryptocurrency.asp
4. https://www.cnb.com/personal-banking/insights/bitcoin-risks-opportunity.html

Chapter 12

The Future of Bitcoin in Financial Systems

In the ever-shifting landscape of the cryptocurrency industry, the destiny of Bitcoin remains a cipher, veiled in uncertainty. Amidst the promises and perils that this technology presents, there lie numerous factors that may exert their influence, potentially reshaping Bitcoin's trajectory. Yet, it is a journey rife with intrigue and boundless possibilities, one that demands a keen eye and an unwavering commitment to adaptation.

One pivotal determinant lies in the crucible of competing cryptocurrencies. Presently, Bitcoin reigns supreme, a colossus towering over the cryptocurrency realm. Its pioneering status, coupled with its robust underlying technology and widespread adoption, has solidified its position as the preeminent digital currency. Yet, it shares the stage with many challenges, each with unique virtues and advantages. Ethereum, with its smart contract capabilities, has carved out a niche as the premier platform for decentralized applications (dApps) and initial coin offerings (ICOs). Ripple, on the other hand, has garnered attention from traditional financial institutions, offering a faster and more efficient cross-border payment solution. As these contenders evolve, refining their features and augmenting their capabilities, they may pose a formidable challenge to Bitcoin's dominion, vying for market share and investor confidence [1].

Simultaneously, the very foundations of the cryptocurrency domain stand poised for transformation, sculpted by the crucible of emerging technologies and financial systems. The advent of quantum computing, for instance, holds the potential to render current cryptographic protocols obsolete, necessitating a paradigm shift in the security measures employed by cryptocurrencies. Similarly, the burgeoning field of artificial intelligence may unveil novel avenues for enhancing the efficiency and scalability of blockchain networks, ushering in a new era of technological prowess. As the crucible of blockchain technology continues to refine and mature, it may forge new economic paradigms that eclipse the current cryptocurrency ecosystem, proffering realms of efficiency and security hitherto uncharted. Traditional financial institutions, too, may unveil their blockchain-based strategies [2], offering a panoply of benefits akin to cryptocurrencies but shorn of the attendant risks and uncertainties.

The drumbeat of regulatory developments is another keynote in the symphony that shall shape Bitcoin's future. Across the globe, governments and regulatory bodies stand at crossroads, some with cautious steps, others with open arms, ushering in a regulatory framework that may either cradle or constrict the growth and evolution of cryptocurrencies. The regulatory milieu [3] in different nations may wield profound sway over the adoption and utilization of Bitcoin and its ilk in the times to come. Clear and well-defined regulations could foster trust and confidence among investors, paving the way for wider mainstream acceptance. Conversely, draconian measures aimed at stifling cryptocurrencies could relegate them to the fringes, relegating their potential to the realm of untapped possibilities.

Moreover, the socio-economic landscape in which Bitcoin operates is ever-evolving. The global financial crisis of 2008 catalyzed the birth of Bitcoin, as it exposed the vulnerabilities of traditional financial systems and fueled a demand for decentralized alternatives. However, as the world navigates through the aftermath of the crisis, and economies stabilize, the impetus for embracing cryptocurrencies may wane. Conversely, if economic turmoil persists [4] or new crises emerge, the allure of Bitcoin and its decentralized nature may be reignited, propelling it to new heights of adoption and utility.

In the outcome, the future of Bitcoin stands as an enigma, an interplay of potentialities, challenges, and uncertainties [5]. Businesses and investors must navigate this intricate terrain with circumspection, meticulously weighing the factors that may shape the trajectory of this technology. Staying abreast of the latest advancements and trends in the cryptocurrency industry is not merely advisable but imperative in making reasonable decisions regarding the future of this transformative technology. Embracing a mindset of adaptability and continuous learning is essential, for the cryptocurrency landscape is as dynamic as it is unpredictable.

1. https://www.investopedia.com/tech/what-will-happen-bitcoin-next-decade/
2. https://www.imf.org/en/Blogs/Articles/2023/02/23/technology-behind-crypto-can-also-improve-payments-providing-a-public-good
3. https://www.linkedin.com/pulse/future-cryptocurrency-regulation-luka-gubo-iotdf/
4. https://www.bis.org/events/eopix_1810/chiu_paper.pdf
5. https://www.eesc.europa.eu/en/our-work/opinions-information-reports/opinions/crypto-assets-challenges-and-opportunities

Chapter 13

Investing in Bitcoin

For those venturing into Bitcoin investment, a compass of prudent considerations is indispensable. While this technology holds the promise of substantial gains, it also unfurls its tapestry of risks and uncertainties, necessitating judicious contemplation before embarking on the voyage of investment.

Foremost among these considerations is the capricious storm of market volatility that characterizes the realm of cryptocurrencies [1]. Here, prices sway and undulate with mercurial caprice, a ballet of gains and losses that demands a steely resolve from investors. Those who tread this path must be prepared to embrace the risk of substantial gains and potentially staggering losses, forging a comfort with this level of volatility as their armor in this market. The very nature of Bitcoin, decentralized and unbound by traditional mechanisms of control, lends itself to this inherent volatility, as market forces shape its trajectory through the ebb and flow of supply and demand.

Another lodestar in the constellation of considerations is the regulatory firmament that enshrouds Bitcoin and its brethren [2]. Across the globe, governments and regulatory bodies assume disparate stances, some treading with caution, others extending open arms, forging a mosaic of regulatory landscapes. To navigate this terrain, investors must remain vigilant, ever watchful of the regulatory winds that may shape the investment climate in different jurisdictions. The uncertainty surrounding the future of cryptocurrency regulation, coupled with the potential for shifting policies, demands a proactive stance from investors, one that prioritizes staying abreast of the latest developments and adapting accordingly.

In parallel, investors must delve into the technical and security underpinnings of Bitcoin with due diligence. Rooted in intricate algorithms and cryptographic protocols, this technology bears potential security risks that must be methodically addressed to safeguard investments. A familiarity and comfort with the technical facets of this technology, coupled with a reasonable selection of reputable exchanges and wallets, is imperative to ensure the sanctity of one's assets. Investors must develop a keen understanding of the mechanics of blockchain technology, the decentralized ledger that underpins Bitcoin, as well as the intricacies of secure storage, transaction verification, and the safeguarding of private keys.

Lastly, a vigilant eye must be cast toward the specter of scams and fraud that can lurk in the shadows of the cryptocurrency market [4]. While there exist numerous upstanding and reputable entities within this domain, a cadre of malefactors seeks to ensnare unwitting investors. Prudent research, due diligence, and a discerning eye are the guardians against falling prey to unscrupulous actors, guiding investors toward legitimate businesses and exchanges. The allure of quick riches and the anonymity afforded by cryptocurrencies can serve as a breeding ground for nefarious activities, necessitating a heightened level of caution and scrutiny from investors.

In summation, Bitcoin investment is a terrain replete with promise but equally fraught with risks and uncertainties [3]. Investors must brace themselves for the capricious tides of gains and losses, forging comfort with the risk profile of this market. By remaining attuned to the latest advancements and trends, investors can chart a course that steers them through the intricate waters of Bitcoin investment, poised to seize the potential opportunities that this technology may proffer. Yet, this journey requires a steadfast commitment to prudence, due diligence, and an unwavering vigilance against the pitfalls that lurk in the shadows of this nascent and ever-evolving landscape.

1. https://www.investopedia.com/investing-in-crypto-6502543
2. https://www.fidelity.com/learning-center/trading-investing/bitcoin-investment-considerations
3. https://www.schwab.com/learn/story/cryptocurrencies-should-you-invest-them
4. https://consumer.ftc.gov/articles/what-know-about-cryptocurrency-and-scams

Chapter 14

Bitcoin's Ripple Effect: Impact on Society and Global Economy

Since its inception, Bitcoin has cast a profound imprint on society and the global economic tapestry. In this chapter, we embark on an odyssey through the various avenues by which Bitcoin has left its indelible mark on culture, as well as its transformative influence on the world economy.

Foremost among Bitcoin's societal impacts is its power to bestow financial inclusion upon those hitherto excluded from the fold of traditional banking services. With a mere internet connection, individuals can now partake in the global economy, circumventing the need for conventional banking intermediaries. This boon is particularly pronounced in regions where access to banking services is constrained or where native currencies oscillate in instability [1]. For the world's unbanked population, long consigned to the peripheries of economic progress, Bitcoin has emerged as a potential emancipator, affording them a gateway into the global financial arena and a means to secure their fiscal sovereignty.

Beyond financial inclusion, Bitcoin has served as a clarion call, summoning attention to the fissures within the prevailing banking edifice. The scars of the 2008 financial crisis and ensuing bailouts, coupled with the opacity and perceived venality of conventional banking practices, have fostered a sense of disenchantment. Bitcoin's decentralized ethos, divorced from the clutches of traditional banks, beckons to those seeking an alternative to the extant system. Its incorruptible, immutable ledger, untethered to the whims of central authorities, has ignited the imaginations of those disillusioned with the status quo, offering a tantalizing vision of a more equitable financial order.

In the crucible of the global economy, Bitcoin's impact is writ large. As more entities and individuals embrace Bitcoin, the citadel of traditional payment systems may quake, potentially eroding the dominion of credit card titans like Visa and Mastercard [3]. The repercussions of this shift may herald diminished transaction costs for both retailers and consumers alike, as Bitcoin bypasses the labyrinthine network of intermediaries that have long reigned over electronic payments [2].

Moreover, Bitcoin bears the potential to metamorphose cross-border payments. Presently, the conduits for sending money across borders are labyrinthine, ensnared in tardiness, exorbitant fees, and the dilemma of currency exchange levies. Bitcoin's decentralized essence, liberated from the constraints of traditional banks, might emerge as a swifter, more cost-effective conduit for international remittances. Its capacity to transcend borders seamlessly, unfettered by the impediments that have historically hampered the flow of funds across nations, could catalyze a revolution in the realm of global finance, democratizing access to cross-border transactions for individuals and businesses alike.

Yet, within this transformative tide, concerns surge. Bitcoin's explosive volatility, fueled by speculation and the whims of market sentiment, has led many to perceive it as a speculative asset rather than a steadfast currency, inciting apprehensions of market destabilization. The lack of an underlying asset or authority to anchor its value has rendered Bitcoin's price trajectory erratic, casting doubts upon its viability as a stable medium of exchange.

Moreover, the absence of oversight and regulation in the Bitcoin sphere has engendered trepidations regarding money laundering and other illicit endeavors. The cloak of anonymity afforded by Bitcoin's decentralized architecture, while preserving user privacy, has also provided fertile ground for nefarious actors to exploit [4] the system for unlawful pursuits. Concerns over the potential misuse of Bitcoin for financing illegal activities have spurred calls for greater regulatory scrutiny and the implementation of robust anti-money laundering measures.

In sum, Bitcoin's imprimatur on society and the global economy is ineffaceable. As the ranks of Bitcoin and other cryptocurrencies swell, the potential for a paradigm shift in our conception of money and finance looms ever more prominent on the horizon. Whether Bitcoin emerges as a disruptive force that reshapes the foundations of global finance or fades into obscurity as a fleeting novelty remains to be seen. Yet, one truth is incontrovertible: the advent of

Bitcoin has catalyzed a profound reckoning with the prevailing financial order, challenging long-held assumptions and paving the way for a future where the concept of money [5] itself may be radically redefined.

1. https://economictimes.indiatimes.com/small-biz/security-tech/technology/bitcoins-price-could-have-a-positive-ripple-effect-on-the-broader-crypto-ecosystem-nftfn/articleshow/108430168.cms?from=mdr
2. https://www.mastercard.com/global/en/business/issuers/crypto/card-program.html
3. https://www.linkedin.com/pulse/embracing-blockchain-visa-mastercard-leading-charge-payment-hzjff/
4. https://www.ccn.com/education/crypto-hacks-exploits-full-list-scams-vulnerabilities/
5. https://www.sciencedirect.com/science/article/pii/S1062976919301528

Chapter 15

Bitcoin's Dark Underbelly: Navigating the Shadows

In the radiant glow of Bitcoin's transformative potential, a shadowy realm teems with unsavory actors seeking to exploit the decentralized sanctuary it provides. This chapter casts a discerning eye on the darker alleys where scams, fraud, and cyber malfeasance loom, cautioning users to tread with vigilance.

Foremost among the nefarious stratagems is the sinister waltz of Ponzi schemes [1], a dance of deceit that promises lavish returns on Bitcoin investments only to pilfer new entrants' contributions to appease earlier investors. This macabre cycle persists until the edifice crumbles, leaving a trail of shattered hopes and empty pockets [2]. The annals of infamy bear testament, from the Mt. Gox fiasco that plundered millions from unsuspecting investors to the OneCoin [3] saga, a grand charade estimated to have absconded with billions. These cautionary tales serve as stark reminders that the siren song of easy riches often cloaks a treacherous undertow.

Yet, the specter of hacking casts an even graver pall. Encrypted within digital wallets, private keys stand sentinel over Bitcoin fortunes, yet malevolent forces have orchestrated audacious heists, pillaging the coffers of exchanges. The 2014 breach of Mt. Gox, which saw the vanishing of $460 million in Bitcoin, and the 2016 Bitfinex [4] raid, netting $72 million, stand as grim epitaphs of this relentless onslaught. Sophisticated cybercriminals, armed with an arsenal of tools, seek to infiltrate the digital vaults that safeguard the cryptocurrency, forever altering the destinies of their unsuspecting victims.

In the annals of Bitcoin's saga, a darker narrative unfolds - one entwined with money laundering and the clandestine bazaars of the dark web. While cash has long been the currency of choice for nefarious deeds, Bitcoin's veiled transactions have drawn in malefactors seeking to cleanse their spoils or procure contraband in the shrouded recesses of the digital realm. The pseudonymity and decentralization that empower Bitcoin's revolutionary ethos have also created a haven for those who would seek to obscure the provenance of their ill-gotten gains or indulge in the trafficking of illicit goods.

Yet, in the face of this shadowed landscape, beacons of prudence illuminate the path forward. Employing reputable exchanges and aegis-laden wallets, guarding private keys as one would a cherished relic, and maintaining an unwavering vigilance for suspicious incursions serve as sentinels against the encroaching darkness. Moreover, governments and enforcement agencies worldwide have heeded the clarion call, taking strides to regulate Bitcoin and its ilk, thereby striking a blow against the proliferation of illicit machinations. The emergence of specialized cybersecurity firms [5] and the implementation of robust compliance measures have also fortified the defenses against those who would seek to exploit the system.

In summation, as Bitcoin's luminous potential converges with the murkier recesses of the digital domain, users must be astute sentinels of their fate. Awareness of the lurking shadows, coupled with reasonable measures, is the crucible that tempers one's foray into this realm. In safeguarding their investments, users stand as bulwarks against the encroachment of scams, fraud, and cyber skullduggery, ensuring that the radiant promise of Bitcoin persists undiminished. Vigilance, discernment, and a steadfast commitment to ethical practices are the hallmarks of those who would harness the power of this revolutionary technology while navigating its darker underbelly.

1. https://www.sec.gov/files/ia_virtualcurrencies.pdf
2. https://www.justice.gov/opa/pr/two-men-charged-operating-25m-cryptocurrency-ponzi-scheme
3. https://www.fbi.gov/wanted/topten/ruja-ignatova/@@download.pdf
4. https://en.wikipedia.org/wiki/Bitfinex
5. https://www.f6s.com/companies/blockchain-security/mo

Chapter 16

The Forks and the Community Divide, starring Bitcoin and its progeny, Bitcoin Cash.

Bitcoin Cash, a digital currency born in the crucible of August 2017, emerged from the minds of developers who dared to fork Bitcoin's blockchain. Their mission: to fashion a new cryptocurrency bedecked with larger block sizes. The crux of the matter lay in a fierce disagreement concerning Bitcoin's trajectory. Specifically, the debate raged on how to expand the network's capacity to embrace a burgeoning hive of users and transactions [1].

The Bitcoin Cash champions championed a cause: they argued for an elevation of Bitcoin's block size, transcending the present confinement of a mere 1MB. Their aim? Swifter, more economic transactions. Yet, the stalwart Bitcoin Core adherents took a divergent stance. They postulated that an augmentation of the block size limit imperiled the sanctity and decentralization of the network.

This schism birthed a hard fork fraught with contention. The outcome? Two distinct cryptocurrencies and their attendant blockchains: Bitcoin (BTC) and Bitcoin Cash (BCH). The rift cleaved the Bitcoin community, casting aspersions of trickery and deceit from one camp to the other [2].

Despite the initial friction, both digital currencies have endured and flourished in their unique manners. Bitcoin reigns supreme, its market cap soaring beyond a trillion dollars as of early 2023. Meanwhile, Bitcoin Cash commands a market capitalization of approximately ten billion dollars and has been welcomed by select vendors as an economical and expedited alternative to its forebear [3].

This fissure also paved the way for other Bitcoin offshoots, such as Bitcoin SV (BSV) and Bitcoin Gold (BTG), each bearing distinct traits and attributes. However, their embrace has been of a different hue compared to the widespread adoption of Bitcoin and Bitcoin Cash.

The gulf in community sentiment between Bitcoin and Bitcoin Cash casts a spotlight on the tribulations of achieving consensus in steering the course of a decentralized network. While the Bitcoin community remains embroiled in block size, the march of progress unveils newfangled technologies and scaling solutions, exemplified by the Lightning Network, potentially offering a reconciliatory path that satiates both camps.

In the aftermath of the fork, the two camps engaged in a fierce battle for the "true" Bitcoin mantle, with each side accusing the other of betraying Satoshi Nakamoto's original vision. The Bitcoin Cash proponents argued that their blockchain remained faithful to the principle of on-chain scaling, while the Bitcoin Core adherents maintained that their approach was necessary to preserve the network's security and decentralization.

The debate extended beyond technical parameters, delving into the realms of ideological allegiance and the future direction of the cryptocurrency ecosystem. The Bitcoin Cash advocates championed the cause of financial inclusion and faster, cheaper transactions, while the Bitcoin Core supporters emphasized the importance of sound money principles and long-term stability.

The rivalry between the two camps manifested in various forms, from social media bickering to hash rate wars, with both sides vying for the support of miners, developers, and the broader cryptocurrency community. The intensity of the conflict highlighted the deep-seated divisions within the Bitcoin ecosystem and the challenges inherent in navigating the delicate balance between scalability, security, and decentralization [4].

As the dust settled, the market capitalization and adoption rates of the two cryptocurrencies provided a tangible reflection of the community's sentiments. Bitcoin's dominance as the market leader and its continued growth underscored the confidence of investors and users in its long-term viability. Conversely, Bitcoin Cash's more modest but steady progress indicated its ability to carve out a niche as an alternative, more transaction-focused cryptocurrency.

The enduring presence of both Bitcoin and Bitcoin Cash, despite the initial schism, highlights the resilience and adaptability of decentralized networks. The ability of these two digital currencies to coexist, each catering to a distinct set of user needs, speaks to the diversity and flexibility inherent in the cryptocurrency landscape.

The fissure between Bitcoin and Bitcoin Cash also paved the way for the emergence of other Bitcoin-derived cryptocurrencies, each with its unique value proposition and approach to the challenges of scalability and governance. While the adoption and success of these offshoots have varied, their very existence underscores the dynamism and innovative spirit that pervades the decentralized finance ecosystem.

In summation, the parting of ways between Bitcoin and Bitcoin Cash [5] etched a seminal chapter in the annals of the cryptocurrency realm, underscoring the tightrope walk between scalability, security, and decentralization. The sustained triumph and expansion of both cryptocurrencies eloquently testify to the tenacity and adaptability of decentralized networks while also affirming the pivotal role of communal consensus in propelling the wheels of innovation and advancement.

As the cryptocurrency industry continues to evolve, the lessons learned from the Bitcoin-Bitcoin Cash divide [6] will undoubtedly shape the future trajectories of the various digital currencies and the underlying blockchain technologies. The ability to navigate these complex trade-offs and foster constructive dialogues within the community will be instrumental in unlocking the full potential of decentralized finance and ensuring its long-term sustainability.

1. https://www.investopedia.com/tech/bitcoin-vs-bitcoin-cash-whats-difference/
2. https://www.ccn.com/education/bitcoin-vs-bitcoin-cash-key-differences/
3. https://www.bitcoin.com/bitcoin-cash-register/
4. https://medium.com/@zifamae/bitcoin-vs-bitcoin-cash-whats-the-difference-between-btc-and-bch-1c641ea0b23f
5. https://www.kraken.com/compare/bitcoin-vs-bitcoin-cash
6. https://finance.yahoo.com/news/btc-vs-bch-investors-split-150000529.html?guccounter=

Chapter 17

The Diverse Landscape of Cryptocurrency: Beyond Bitcoin's Horizon

In the grand tapestry of cryptocurrencies, Bitcoin stands as the undisputed titan, reigning supreme in market capitalization and user adoption. Yet, the stage is no longer solely reserved for this behemoth. With Bitcoin's meteoric ascent, a constellation of alternative cryptocurrencies, affectionately dubbed altcoins, has burst forth. These digital currencies bear the mantle of addressing perceived vulnerabilities within Bitcoin while ushering in novel functionalities and features.

Amongst this constellation, Ethereum gleams as one of the brightest stars, its inception dating back to 2015. Crafted to be a versatile blockchain platform, Ethereum extends an open invitation to developers, urging them to weave smart contracts [1] and forge decentralized applications [2]. This unique prowess has anointed Ethereum as the preferred launchpad for myriad ICOs (Initial Coin Offerings), igniting the flame of funding that has kindled billions for nascent blockchain ventures. The rise of Ethereum has been meteoric, with its market capitalization soaring to rival even that of Bitcoin in recent years, solidifying its position as a force to be reckoned with in the cryptocurrency landscape.

Another luminary in the pantheon of Bitcoin alternatives is Ripple. It is tailored for swifter and more efficient cross-border transactions. Ripple's distinctive feature lies in its embrace of a consensus algorithm, forsaking the conventional proof-of-work [3] paradigm. This shift quickens the pulse of transaction times and trims down the toll of fees. Ripple has found success in partnering with traditional financial institutions, enabling seamless integration with existing banking infrastructure, a feat that has garnered significant attention and adoption within the financial sector.

Further along the sky, we encounter Litecoin, a fleet-footed contender born to outpace Bitcoin's strides in speed and efficiency. Designed as a "silver" to Bitcoin's "gold," Litecoin has carved out a niche for itself, offering faster transaction times and lower fees, making it an attractive option for smaller, everyday transactions [4]. The steady rise of Litecoin's user base and its growing acceptance as a viable payment method have solidified its position as a prominent altcoin.

Then, there is Bitcoin Cash, a progeny of a seismic hard fork in the blockchain in 2017. Its mission? To widen the boulevards of the Bitcoin blockchain, paving the way for expedited transactions and diminished fees. Bitcoin Cash has been the subject of much debate [5] within the cryptocurrency community, with proponents arguing that it remains true to the original vision of Bitcoin, while critics claim it has diverged too far from the core principles.

These altcoins, each bearing distinct virtues, are not without their trials. Many grapple with the elusive prize of mainstream recognition and adoption while the cryptocurrency market at large conducts a symphony of volatility. Moreover, some altcoins have been entangled in accusations of cheating or pyramid-like machinations [6], casting a shadow of skepticism over discerning investors' quest for legitimacy.

Yet, in the face of these tribulations, the ascendance of alternative cryptocurrencies stands as a testament to the enduring allure of the blockchain bedrock beneath them. As a legion of developers and visionaries persist in probing the uncharted realms of blockchain technology, we can reasonably anticipate the continued emergence of fresh cryptocurrencies poised to challenge the dominion of Bitcoin in the epochs yet to unfold. The future of cryptocurrency is not limited to a single contender, but rather a diverse and thriving ecosystem, where innovation and disruption reign supreme.

1. https://www.quicknode.com/guides/ethereum-development/smart-contracts/an-overview-of-how-smart-contracts-work-on-ethereum
2. https://www.alchemy.com/ecosystem/ethereum
3. https://www.forbes.com/advisor/investing/cryptocurrency/proof-of-work/
4. https://worldcoin.org/articles/what-is-litecoin
5. https://www.securities.io/investing-in-bitcoin-cash/
6. https://finance.yahoo.com/news/cryptocurrencies-being-savaged-davos-top-123512836.html

Chapter 18

Navigating the Legal Labyrinth: Bitcoin and Regulatory Realities

In the captivating world of cryptocurrency, Bitcoin's unmoored nature, devoid of traditional regulatory shackles, presents a dual-edged sword. On one hand, it grants users heightened financial autonomy and privacy, a boon for those seeking greater control over their financial lives. Yet, this very quality unfurls a vexing tapestry for governments and regulatory bodies as they grapple with reining in and overseeing the burgeoning usage of Bitcoin.

Across the global landscape, the legal standing of Bitcoin paints a diverse and ever-evolving panorama. Countries like Japan and Australia have extended a welcoming hand, legalizing Bitcoin and bestowing upon it the coveted mantle of currency. Contrastingly, nations like China and Russia have sounded the gong of outright prohibition, decreeing Bitcoin persona non grata within their borders. In the United States, the legal stance on Bitcoin remains in a perpetual state of flux, with the regulatory scaffold evolving in a constant dance, seeking to keep pace with this disruptive digital asset.

Among the myriad trials confronting Bitcoin is its potential entanglement in illicit pursuits, ranging from money laundering [1] to the nefarious financing of terrorism. This has catalyzed heightened vigilance from regulatory quarters, prompting many nations to enact stringent anti-money laundering (AML) and know-your-customer (KYC) edicts for Bitcoin exchanges and associated enterprises. These measures aim to bring greater transparency and accountability to the Bitcoin ecosystem, yet they also threaten to erode some of the very qualities that have endeared it to its ardent supporters.

In the United States, the Financial Crimes Enforcement Network (FinCEN [2]) stands as the sentinel, orchestrating the regulation of Bitcoin. In 2013, FinCEN issued a clarion call, stipulating that virtual currency exchanges and administrators be anointed as money transmitters, thereby falling under the purview of AML and KYC norms. By 2015, FinCEN had wielded its punitive hand, exacting penalties against a prominent Bitcoin exchange for flouting these crucial AML statutes.

The Internal Revenue Service (IRS [3]), too, has cast its gaze upon Bitcoin, deeming it property for taxation purposes. In 2014, the IRS issued directives affirming that Bitcoin transactions are firmly trapped within the web of capital gains tax. Those who partake in the buying and selling of Bitcoin are now duty-bound to chronicle their transactions meticulously and tender taxes on any accrued gains, further complicating the landscape for Bitcoin users.

Yet another hurdle facing Bitcoin is the clarion call for greater transparency concerning its legal footing in select jurisdictions. This demand for clarity has heralded high-profile cases wherein Bitcoin users have found themselves in the crosshairs, accused of crimes ranging from money laundering to drug trafficking. In some instances, Bitcoin has served as an evidentiary linchpin, bolstering charges; in others, it has been confiscated as a pawn in criminal investigations [4], further muddying the waters of its legal status.

Despite these arduous trials and tribulations, Bitcoin's star continues to ascend, etching its indelible mark upon the global economic tableau. As an ever-expanding cadre of enterprises and individuals embrace this digital currency, governments and regulatory bodies are poised to refine their approach to its governance further. The trajectory of Bitcoin remains nebulous, yet its potential to reshape the very foundations of the financial landscape stands as an indisputable truth. The dance between innovation and regulation continues [5], with the future of Bitcoin hanging in the delicate balance.

1. https://www.chainalysis.com/blog/2024-crypto-money-laundering/
2. https://www.fincen.gov/
3. https://www.irs.gov/businesses/small-businesses-self-employed/digital-assets
4. https://syntheticdrugs.unodc.org/syntheticdrugs/en/cybercrime/detectandrespond/investigation/cryptocurrency.html

5. https://www.britannica.com/money/cryptocurrency-regulation

Chapter 19

Bitcoin and Blockchain: A Dance of Technological Titans

In the annals of the 21st century, two titans emerge, bearing the transformation standard: Bitcoin and blockchain. Bitcoin, a decentralized digital currency, forges its path on a peer-to-peer network, eschewing the need for intermediaries. Complementing this, blockchain, a distributed ledger marvel, lays the bedrock for Bitcoin and a plethora of other cryptocurrencies. While distinct, their destinies are entwined, with blockchain as the bedrock for Bitcoin's decentralized ethos and furnishing the scaffold for a cornucopia of blockchain-driven applications.

The genesis of Bitcoin unfurls in the wake of a white paper birthed in 2008. Its author is shrouded in the enigma of the pseudonym Satoshi Nakamoto. This treatise envisions a novel digital currency orchestrated on a decentralized network, fortified by the bulwark of cryptography, guarding against skullduggery.

At the heart of this marvel lies blockchain, a distributed ledger, an impervious tome chronicling all network transactions with transparency and invulnerability to tampering. Blockchain's decentralized nature ensures that no single entity controls the network, fostering trust and security. Each transaction is recorded on a distributed network of computers, with copies of the ledger maintained by multiple nodes. This decentralized approach eliminates the need for a central authority, such as a bank or government, to validate and record transactions, reducing the risk of fraud and corruption [1].

While Bitcoin heralded the dawn of blockchain, its legacy now spans diverse industries, from finance and supply chain management to healthcare and even the burgeoning world of non-fungible tokens (NFTs) [2]. Blockchain, with its decentralized, transparent, and inviolable essence, emerges as the linchpin for establishing trusted networks, ushering in transactions sans intermediaries.

At the heart of blockchain's prowess is its capacity to conquer intermediaries and pare down transaction costs. In traditional financial echelons, intermediaries such as banks and third-party service providers reign as indispensable conduits. Yet, their presence exacts a toll, particularly in cross-border transactions. Blockchain rewrites this narrative, allowing parties to transact directly, unfettered by intermediaries, on a decentralized network. This disintermediation not only reduces costs but also streamlines the transaction process, making it faster and more efficient.

Transparency [3] and security constitute another citadel of blockchain's dominion. Transactions etch their indelible mark on a public ledger, a tapestry accessible to all network participants, impervious to manipulation by any lone actor. Additionally, cryptographic algorithms [4] stand sentinel, safeguarding transactions and ensuring that only duly authorized entities wield the power to access and modify the data. This robust security framework has made blockchain an attractive option for applications that require high levels of trust and data integrity, such as supply chain management, digital identity verification, and even voting systems.

The pas de deux between Bitcoin and blockchain is a saga in perpetual motion, each informing and sculpting the evolution of the other. While Bitcoin commands the limelight as the vanguard of blockchain technology, its application horizons stretch far and wide. As blockchain matures and evolves, its potential becomes a harbinger of transformation across various industries, spanning finance, healthcare, supply chain management, and beyond.

In the realm of finance, blockchain-based platforms [5] are revolutionizing the way transactions are processed, securities are traded, and financial products are structured. The transparency and immutability of the blockchain ledger have made it an ideal foundation for digital asset exchanges, peer-to-peer lending, and decentralized finance (DeFi) applications. Similarly, in the healthcare sector, blockchain is being explored for secure data sharing, clinical trial management, and supply chain traceability of pharmaceutical products.

Beyond finance and healthcare, blockchain is also making inroads in the world of supply chain management. By providing a transparent and tamper-proof record of transactions, blockchain can enhance visibility, traceability, and accountability throughout the supply chain. This has led to applications in areas such as food safety, product provenance, and ethical sourcing.

In summation, the ascent of Bitcoin and blockchain reshapes our understanding of currency, trust, and security. While hurdles persist, the promise held within these technologies looms too significant to be ignored. As we continue to plumb the depths of the interplay between Bitcoin and blockchain, we stand poised to witness the emergence of even more transformative applications in the years ahead. The potential of these technologies to disrupt and transform industries, empower individuals, and foster a more transparent and secure global ecosystem is a compelling vision that will continue to captivate innovators, entrepreneurs, and policymakers alike.

1. https://www.ibm.com/topics/blockchain-security
2. https://www.entrepreneur.com/money-finance/why-nfts-will-make-a-comeback-in-2024/469664
3. https://hashstudioz.com/blog/how-does-blockchain-technology-ensure-transparency-in-cryptocurrency-trade/
4. https://blog.cfte.education/what-is-cryptography-in-blockchain/
5. https://fintechmagazine.com/crypto/top-10-blockchain-platforms

Chapter 20

Bitcoin and Political Ideals: A Canvas of Libertarianism, Anarchism, and More

Bitcoin, a beacon of decentralized finance, has woven itself into the fabric of political ideologies centered on personal liberty and emancipation from governmental sway. In this chapter, we embark on a journey to uncover the political bedrock of Bitcoin and how its decentralized essence harmonizes with specific ideological tenets.

Libertarianism [1], a creed championing individual autonomy and advocating for minimal governmental intervention, has emerged as a favored ideology among fans of Bitcoin. For many early adopters, Bitcoin represented a means to sidestep government hegemony over financial systems, an avenue to forge an authentically liberated market. The Libertarian Party in the United States stood at the vanguard, becoming one of the inaugural political entities to embrace Bitcoin donations for their campaigns. Prominent Libertarian figures, such as Ron Paul [2] and Gary Johnson [3], have long championed the virtues of Bitcoin as a tool for economic emancipation, resonating with their party's core principles of limited government and free-market capitalism.

Anarchism, another political philosophy heralding the abolition of governance and hierarchy, has likewise intertwined its destiny with Bitcoin. Within this sphere, anarcho-capitalists carve their niche, endorsing a capitalist economic framework devoid of governmental intervention. To them, Bitcoin emerges as a conduit for realizing their vision of a society devoid of state apparatus. They posit that Bitcoin's decentralized fabric renders it the quintessential currency for individuals to transact sans government intrusion, creating a voluntary, self-regulating economic order. Anarchist thinkers, such as Murray Rothbard [4] and David Friedman [5], have hailed Bitcoin as a technological breakthrough that aligns with their ideals of a stateless, market-driven society.

Yet, it is imperative to recognize that not all proponents and users of Bitcoin espouse these particular beliefs. The allure of Bitcoin's decentralization and emancipation from government strictures may beckon individuals for various reasons—ranging from concerns regarding privacy to a profound distrust of traditional financial institutions or, perhaps, an intrinsic fascination with the technological marvel. Some see Bitcoin as a means to champion economic freedom without necessarily aligning with Libertarian or Anarchist ideologies, but rather as a tool to promote financial inclusion and empowerment for the unbanked and underserved.

Nonetheless, the juncture of Bitcoin and politics is entangled in a web of contention. Critics have slammed the utilization of Bitcoin for political contributions [6], contending that it may serve as a conduit for illicit activities or a means to subvert campaign finance regulations. Moreover, Bitcoin's decentralized character has rendered it a challenging quarry for governmental oversight, kindling apprehensions regarding its potential for money laundering and other illicit undertakings. Policymakers and regulators have grappled with the task of striking a balance between fostering innovation and mitigating risks, as they navigate the uncharted terrain of cryptocurrencies.

The dalliance between Bitcoin and political ideologies is a continuum, an ever-evolving tapestry. As the technology marches forward, its political ramifications are poised to deepen in complexity and diversity. The outcome—whether Bitcoin shall ultimately serve as a catalyst to challenge established political paradigms or assimilate into their ranks—remains an enigma yet to be unraveled. The future interplay between Bitcoin and the political landscape [7] promises to be a captivating and consequential journey, one that will undoubtedly shape the contours of our economic and social fabric in the years to come.

1. https://www.libertarianism.org/topics/bitcoin
2. https://www.politico.com/news/magazine/2022/04/05/ron-paul-crypto-00022354
3. https://www.calcbench.com/blog/post/167746799503/talking-about-bitcoin
4. https://mises.org/profile/murray-n-rothbard

5. https://podcasts.apple.com/us/podcast/david-friedman-dating-markets-legal-systems-bitcoin/id1516093381?i=1000531485801
6. https://www.fec.gov/help-candidates-and-committees/filing-reports/bitcoin-contributions/
7. https://www.reuters.com/world/us/super-tuesday-test-resurgent-crypto-industrys-political-might-2024-03-03/

Chapter 21

Bitcoin's Dual Persona: Currency or Store of Value?

Since its inception, Bitcoin has donned the mantle of a digital currency, a decentralized form of monetary exchange liberated from intermediaries like traditional banks. Yet, as the value of Bitcoin ascended to stratospheric heights in the years that followed its genesis, its utility as a currency has been cast into the crucible of doubt. Instead, a growing cohort now perceives Bitcoin through the lens of a store of value akin to precious commodities such as gold [1].

This dichotomy has sparked a vigorous debate among economists, investors, and enthusiasts of cryptocurrency alike, revolving around the pivotal question: should Bitcoin be classified as a currency or a store of value? [2] Advocates posit that Bitcoin's decentralized essence and efficacy as a medium of exchange render it a bona fide currency. Detractors, however, point to its rampant volatility and limited payment acceptance, branding it as subpar money.

They assert that its value is predominantly fueled by speculation and fervor.

One of the difficulties in delineating Bitcoin's classification stems from its multifaceted nature as both a currency and an asset. In stark contrast to conventional currencies, like the US dollar, tethered to the auspices of governments and subject to the sway of central banks, Bitcoin thrives independently of any centralized authority. This renders it impervious to inflation and the clutch of governmental interventions—an attribute that prompts many investors to revere it as a store of value.

Simultaneously, the erratic fluctuations in Bitcoin's value bestow upon it the mantle of a precarious investment [3]. Moreover, its limited adoption as a means of payment underscores the imperative for improvement in its utility as a currency. While some enterprises and retailers have leaped to embrace Bitcoin in their transactional repertoire, its diffusion has been a measured process, with a long road ahead before it assumes a prominent role in everyday commerce.

Another problem in characterizing Bitcoin lies in its diversification of purpose, extending beyond its role as a mere currency. The blockchain technology that underpins Bitcoin has birthed a realm of decentralized applications, or dApps, allowing users to construct and operate applications atop the Bitcoin network. This facet has prompted some to view Bitcoin less as a currency or asset and more as a bastion of innovation—a platform poised to reshape industries.

In the final analysis, the debate regarding Bitcoin's identity will persist. While some perceive it predominantly as a currency, others envision it as a repository of value or a crucible for innovation. As the landscape of Bitcoin and other cryptocurrencies evolves, their true essence may come into sharper focus. For now, the debate rages on, a testament to the dynamic nature of this groundbreaking technology.

Additionally, the future trajectory of Bitcoin's development could further influence its classification. Ongoing efforts to improve its scalability, transaction speed, and price stability may enhance its viability as a currency [4]. Conversely, the emergence of new use cases and applications leveraging the Bitcoin network could solidify its standing as a store of value or a technological platform. The resolution of this debate may hinge on the ability of Bitcoin to strike a balance between its dual personas and address the shortcomings that have sparked this discussion in the first place.

1. https://finance.yahoo.com/news/bitcoin-vs-gold-one-better-183000330.html
2. https://www.researchgate.net/publication/350347038_Should_Bitcoin_Be_Classified_as_Money
3. https://www.nerdwallet.com/article/investing/is-bitcoin-a-good-investment
4. https://www.nber.org/system/files/working_papers/w19747/w19747.pdf

Chapter 22

Bitcoin's Embrace: Fostering Financial Inclusion in the Developing World

In the tapestry of financial technology, Bitcoin emerges as a beacon of promise, poised to revolutionize conventional fiscal paradigms. Among its most profound pledges lies the prospect of extending financial inclusivity to the unbanked and underbanked populations in the developing world.

Across vast expanses, traditional banking services remain distant dreams, elusive or nonexistent. The unbanked find themselves tethered to informal financial channels; avenues are fraught with high costs and difficult uncertainties. Bitcoin, with its decentralized ethos and global reach, stands as a potential bridge across this chasm, offering financial services to those left on the fringes.

Central to Bitcoin's prowess is its emancipation from the need for a conventional banking infrastructure. With a smartphone and an internet connection, anyone can partake in the global economic tableau. This means that even those residing in the farthest reaches of the world can engage in economic activity without dependence on traditional banking institutions. This democratization of finance has the power to transform lives, empowering individuals and communities that have long been marginalized from the formal financial system [1].

Numerous developing nations have embraced Bitcoin as a means to champion financial inclusion. Countries like Kenya [2] and Tanzania [3] have harnessed Bitcoin to deliver financial services to those previously excluded. In these regions, Bitcoin facilitates remittances, grants access to credit, and even promotes the purchase of essential goods and services. The impact has been profound, as Bitcoin enables individuals to securely store and transfer funds, access capital, and participate in the global economy without the constraints of traditional banking.

Moreover, Bitcoin has catalyzed economic progress in select developing nations. In Venezuela [4], where hyperinflation has plagued the local currency, Bitcoin has emerged as a sanctuary of value, a bastion for safeguarding wealth. In Zimbabwe [5], Bitcoin has been an instrument to circumvent government constraints on foreign exchange, propelling international trade and economic activity. These use cases demonstrate the transformative potential of Bitcoin in regions where conventional financial systems have failed to meet the needs of the people.

Yet, challenges exist on the road to widespread Bitcoin adoption in the developing world. Foremost among them is the imperative for more excellent education and awareness about Bitcoin. Many residents of developing nations are still strangers to Bitcoin, necessitating comprehensive education on its secure and prudent usage. This will be crucial in building trust and fostering widespread adoption, as individuals must understand the benefits and risks associated with using this new financial technology.

Infrastructure to support Bitcoin transactions is another critical challenge. While Bitcoin may eschew the need for a traditional banking infrastructure, it does hinge upon a dependable internet connection and access to a smartphone or computer. In many parts of the developing world, these resources still need to be more widely available. Investments in digital infrastructure and increased access to digital devices will be essential in unlocking the full potential of Bitcoin in these regions.

Lastly, regulatory ambiguity poses a hurdle. Governments in the developing world grapple with how to regulate Bitcoin and other cryptocurrencies. Some extend open arms, while others slam doors shut. This uncertainty can create a climate where businesses and individuals tread cautiously in utilizing Bitcoin. Clear and enabling regulatory frameworks will be crucial in fostering an environment conducive to Bitcoin's growth and adoption.

1. https://researchfdi.com/resources/articles/rising-popularity-cryptocurrencies-developing-countries/

2. https://www.businessdailyafrica.com/bd/economy/kenya-moves-to-regulate-bitcoin-trade-on-grey-listing-risk--4529684
3. https://bowmanslaw.com/insights/the-ban-on-cryptocurrency-in-tanzania/
4. https://www.forbes.com/sites/eliasferrerbreda/2024/03/06/venezuelas-crypto-rebirth-interview-with-enrique-de-los-reyes/
5. https://www.forbes.com/sites/martinrivers/2022/07/27/bitcoin-could-solve-zimbabwes-hyperinflation-problem--instead-the-country-is-telling-impoverished-citizens-to-just-buy-gold/

Chapter 23

Bitcoin Wallets: Varieties and Operations

Bitcoin wallets are digital gatekeepers, enabling users to store, send, and receive bitcoins. There exists a diverse array of Bitcoin wallet types, each wielding its unique strengths and drawbacks. In this chapter, we will journey through the manifold varieties of Bitcoin wallets and their functionalities in greater detail.

Hardware Wallets
At the vanguard of security, hardware wallets manifest as physical devices designed to harbor bitcoins offline. Unplugged from the internet, they stand fortified against hacking attempts, making them the most secure option for storing large amounts of cryptocurrency. Typically, a hardware wallet is a USB stick adorned with a modest screen displaying vital information. Access requires the user to input a PIN code, introducing an additional layer of security. This makes hardware wallets an ideal choice for long-term storage of bitcoins, as they are impervious to online threats. Prominent examples of hardware wallets encompass Ledger and Trezor, which have gained widespread popularity among cryptocurrency enthusiasts [1].

Software Wallets
Dwelling in the digital realm, software wallets find their abode on devices such as computers or smartphones.

Accessible online, they are the vanguards of everyday transactions, providing users with a convenient way to manage their bitcoins. Software wallets cleave into two distinct categories:

Desktop Wallets
Desktop wallets unfurl as software packages that users download and install on their computers. They bequeath complete control over bitcoins by storing private keys locally, offering a higher level of security compared to web wallets. Desktop wallets also provide more advanced features, such as the ability to customize transaction fees and access advanced transaction history. Esteemed exemplars of desktop wallets encompass Electrum and Exodus, which have earned a reputation for their user-friendly interfaces and robust security features [2].

Mobile Wallets
Mobile wallets take residence as applications downloadable on smartphones. They furnish users with the ability to store and employ bitcoins while on the move, making them a popular choice for everyday transactions. Mobile wallets, though convenient, necessitate enhanced security measures due to potential vulnerabilities in smartphone security. Users should exercise caution when utilizing mobile wallets, ensuring that their device is properly secured and that they are using a reputable wallet provider. Eminent instances of mobile wallets comprise Mycelium and Breadwallet, which offer features like biometric authentication and seamless integration with mobile payment systems [3].

Web Wallets

Web wallets materialize as online vaults accessible through a web browser. Typically hosted by a third-party provider, they grant users entry to their bitcoins through a login and password. Convenience is their forte, as they allow for easy access to one's cryptocurrency holdings from any internet-connected device. However, they are deemed the least secure due to their reliance on third parties for private key storage, making them vulnerable to hacking attempts and provider failures. Users should exercise caution when utilizing web wallets and consider them only for small, short-term holdings. Paradigmatic instances of web wallets encompass Coinbase and Blockchain.info, which have gained popularity for their user-friendly interfaces and integration with fiat currency exchanges [4].

Paper Wallets

Paper wallets manifest as tangible renditions of a Bitcoin wallet's private key. They can be printed on paper or generated through a software program. Paper wallets ascend as the pinnacle of security, existing in splendid isolation from the internet. However, they also entail the most significant inconvenience, necessitating manual input of the private key for transactions. This makes paper wallets an ideal choice for long-term storage of large amounts of bitcoins, as they are immune to online threats. Users must exercise extreme caution when generating and storing paper wallets, as the loss or damage of the physical document could result in the permanent loss of their bitcoins. Paper wallets offer the highest level of security but at the expense of convenience [5].

In summation, the selection of a Bitcoin wallet hinges on the user's specific requisites and preferences. Hardware wallets reign supreme in security, while software wallets may be more suitable for everyday transactions. Desktop and mobile wallets, though elegant and user-friendly, may cede some speed to hardware wallets. Web wallets, while fit for daily transactions, occupy the lowest rung in terms of security. Paper wallets offer the pinnacle of security but at the expense of convenience. Thorough research and selecting a reputable wallet provider are crucial to safeguarding one's bitcoins, as the choice of wallet can have significant implications for the security and accessibility of one's cryptocurrency holdings.

1. https://www.coinbureau.com/analysis/best-hardware-wallets/
2. https://www.coinbureau.com/review/best-crypto-desktop-wallets/
3. https://money.com/best-crypto-wallets/
4. https://www.capterra.com/cryptocurrency-wallets-software/s/web-based/
5. https://www.investopedia.com/terms/p/paper-wallet.asp

Chapter 24

Bitcoin's Cultural Resonance

Beyond the realms of finance, Bitcoin has permeated popular culture, leaving an indelible mark on movies, TV shows, music, art, and even video games. As this digital currency has gained widespread recognition and adoption, its influence has transcended the boundaries of the financial world, resonating with various creative and artistic mediums.

In the cinematic sphere, Bitcoin and cryptocurrencies have assumed diverse portrayals, reflecting the multifaceted nature of this revolutionary technology. The 2015 film "Dope" [1] stands out as a notable example, weaving a narrative around a group of teenagers inadvertently entangled in a trove of Bitcoin, thrust into the dangerous landscape of cryptocurrency. Here, Bitcoin emerges as a high-stakes venture and a beacon of financial emancipation, capturing the imagination of audiences and exploring the societal implications of this decentralized digital currency.

The acclaimed TV series "Mr. Robot" [2] grants Bitcoin a pivotal role in its storyline, showcasing the currency's potential for disruption within the financial ecosystem. Protagonist Elliot employs Bitcoin as a cornerstone in his hacking endeavors, using it as a tool to challenge the status quo and expose the flaws in the traditional financial system.

In the realm of music, Bitcoin finds its voice, resonating with artists who have embraced its transformative potential. Renowned rapper Nas, a fervent advocate of Bitcoin, has even co-founded a venture capital firm dedicated to cryptocurrency startups. His 2014 track "The Season" [3] echoes the sentiment, alluding to Bitcoin's capacity to empower individuals and disrupt the established financial order.

The artistic community has also drawn inspiration from the enigmatic allure of Bitcoin. Federico Clapis' sculpture "Crypto Connection" [4] poignantly captures the nexus between technology and human cognition, depicting a human brain adorned with Bitcoin insignia. This work serves as a thought-provoking exploration of how Bitcoin and blockchain technology have the potential to reshape our understanding of finance, identity, and the very fabric of society.

Even the realm of video games bears witness to Bitcoin's influence, as exemplified by the popular title "Bitcoin Billionaire." [5] In this game, players partake in the virtual pursuit of mining Bitcoins and amassing a digital fortune, captivating crypto enthusiasts and gamers alike. This virtual experience not only entertains but also educates players about the intricacies of cryptocurrency and the potential for wealth creation in the digital age.

The ubiquity of Bitcoin in popular culture attests to its burgeoning impact and relevance in the global landscape. As cryptocurrency familiarity continues to burgeon, we can anticipate Bitcoin and blockchain technology to continue gracing various forms of media, further cementing their place in contemporary culture. From the silver screen to the recording studio, and from the art gallery to the virtual world, Bitcoin's influence is undeniable, serving as a testament to its transformative power and the profound impact it is having on the collective consciousness of our time.

1. https://www.imdb.com/title/tt3850214/
2. https://www.rottentomatoes.com/tv/mr_robot
3. https://genius.com/Nas-the-season-lyrics
4. https://www.forbes.com/sites/eidoo/2018/06/18/london-hosts-worlds-first-public-crypto-sculpture-crypto-connection-commissioned-by-eidoo/
5. https://noodlecake.com/games/bitcoin-billionaire/

Chapter 25

Bitcoin Software Infrastructure

Bitcoin, operating in a decentralized realm bereft of central authorities or intermediaries, relies on a network of nodes for transaction verification. Any individual can partake in this network, joining the ranks of transaction validators. At the heart of Bitcoin's operations lies a fusion of cryptography and computer science, with software playing a pivotal role.

Bitcoin software implementation encompasses an array of programs and tools instrumental in establishing, managing, and running the Bitcoin network. This includes client software for end-users and server software for nodes and mining pools. Various types of Bitcoin software exist, each wielding distinctive features and functionalities.

Foremost among these is the Bitcoin Core client [1], widely adopted and maintained by the Bitcoin Core development team. As open-source software, its development is open to contributions from the community, and it is available for download from the Bitcoin Core website. Functioning as a full node client, it entails the download and upkeep of a complete blockchain. This client serves as the reference implementation for the Bitcoin protocol, providing a reliable and secure platform for users to interact with the network.

In contrast, lightweight clients prioritize speed and efficiency over comprehensive blockchain downloads. They eschew the need for whole blockchain storage, relying on other nodes for transaction verification. Notable examples include Electrum [2], MultiBit [3], and Armory [4]. These lightweight clients are particularly useful for mobile devices or users with limited storage space, as they offer a more streamlined and user-friendly experience.

Beyond client software, the Bitcoin network relies on various server software implementations. These encompass Bitcoin Unlimited [5], Bitcoin Classic (that will close soon)[6], and Bitcoin XT [7]. Nodes and mining pools leverage these server software programs to verify transactions and forge new blocks. These alternative implementations often introduce innovative features or propose modifications to the core Bitcoin protocol, contributing to the ongoing evolution and improvement of the network.

Integral to Bitcoin's software implementation is the consensus mechanism governing transaction validation and blockchain extension. This mechanism hinges on a proof-of-work algorithm, mandating miners to solve intricate mathematical puzzles for transaction validation and block addition—a process known as mining [8]. In turn, miners are rewarded with freshly minted bitcoins. This consensus mechanism ensures the integrity and security of the blockchain by incentivizing miners to contribute their computational resources to the network.

Supplementary software tools and applications augment Bitcoin's ecosystem. Wallets are repositories for storing and managing bitcoins, with a diverse range of options catering to different user preferences and security requirements. These wallets, such as hardware wallets, mobile wallets, and desktop wallets, provide secure and user-friendly interfaces for users to manage their digital assets.

Furthermore, APIs enable developers to craft applications interfacing with the Bitcoin network, unlocking a world of innovation and ecosystem expansion. These APIs facilitate the integration of Bitcoin functionality into a wide range of applications, from payment processors to financial services and beyond. [9]

Additionally, software tools for monitoring Bitcoin price trends, analyzing market dynamics, and making informed trading decisions further enrich the ecosystem. These analytics and trading platforms empower users to gain valuable insights and make data-driven decisions in the volatile and rapidly evolving cryptocurrency market. [10]

1. https://bitcoin.org/en/bitcoin-core/
2. https://electrum.org/
3. https://multibit.exchange/

4. https://btcarmory.com/
5. https://www.bitcoinunlimited.info/
6. https://bitcoinclassic.com/news/closing.html
7. https://github.com/bitcoinxt/bitcoinxt?tab=readme-ov-file
8. https://www.nerdwallet.com/article/investing/bitcoin-mining
9. https://www.blockchain.com/explorer/api
10. https://medium.com/coinmonks/12-best-blockchain-analysis-tools-2fb8bd62db5c

Chapter 26

The Blockchain: Verifying and Recording Bitcoin Transactions

The blockchain, the bedrock of Bitcoin and various cryptocurrencies, is a distributed ledger technology. It forms an indelible, public record of every transaction executed on the network. This decentralized database diverges from the conventional model by dispersing information across a network of computers rather than centralizing it on a solitary server. [1]

Bitcoin transactions undergo verification and recording on the blockchain through a process known as mining. Miners employ potent computers to tackle intricate mathematical challenges, appending new blocks of transactions to the blockchain. In return for their efforts, miners receive freshly minted bitcoins and transaction fees. The mining process is essential to the security and integrity of the blockchain, as it ensures that all transactions are verified and added to the permanent record. [2]

Each block within the blockchain encompasses a series of transactions validated by the network. Once integrated into the blockchain, a block becomes unalterable and impervious to deletion without achieving consensus from the network. This characteristic imbues the blockchain with unparalleled security, ensuring it is an incorruptible record of all transactions. The immutability of the blockchain is a key feature that has garnered significant interest and adoption across various industries. [3]

Operating on a peer-to-peer network, every node maintains a copy of the blockchain. This decentralized architecture precludes any single entity from exerting control. It also means that even if one node falters or is compromised, the network as a whole continues to operate seamlessly. This distributed nature of the blockchain provides a high level of resilience and redundancy, making it resistant to single points of failure.

A defining attribute of the blockchain is its transparency [4]. The entirety of the blockchain, along with all transactions on the network, is accessible for public scrutiny. This high transparency confers significant trust and accountability to Bitcoin and other cryptocurrencies. Transparency also enables the tracing and verification of transactions, which is crucial for regulatory compliance and anti-money laundering efforts.

Beyond Bitcoin, the blockchain boasts a multitude of potential applications. It can authenticate identities, trace supply chains, and facilitate decentralized applications. Furthermore, the blockchain is under exploration for enhancing voting systems and curbing fraud in elections [5]. The ability to record and verify transactions without the need for a central authority has made the blockchain an attractive solution for various industries, including finance, supply chain management, and government administration.

The blockchain stands as a revolutionary force that can reshape numerous industries. Its decentralized and transparent character renders it an enticing solution for a diverse array of applications. As time progresses, we can anticipate a surge of innovations and advancements in this transformative technology, with the potential to disrupt established practices and introduce new paradigms of trust, transparency, and efficiency.

1. https://www.ibm.com/topics/blockchain

2. https://freemanlaw.com/mining-explained-a-detailed-guide-on-how-cryptocurrency-mining-works/
3. https://www.chainalysis.com/blog/blockchain-security/
4. https://link.springer.com/article/10.1007/s12525-022-00536-0
5. https://www.mdpi.com/2079-9292/13/1/17

Chapter 27

Bitcoin Trading: How to Buy and Sell Bitcoins

Bitcoin trading involves the buying and selling of Bitcoin to profit from price changes in the cryptocurrency market. Similar to trading stocks or currencies, it requires an understanding of the fundamentals and various strategies to navigate the dynamic world of digital assets. In this expanded chapter, we will delve deeper into the process of buying and selling Bitcoin, explore the different types of exchanges, and discuss several popular trading strategies.

Buying Bitcoin [1]

The first step in Bitcoin trading is acquiring the cryptocurrency itself. There are several methods available:

Bitcoin Exchanges: These online platforms facilitate the buying and selling of Bitcoin using fiat currency or other cryptocurrencies. Prominent exchanges include Coinbase, Binance, Kraken, and Gemini. These exchanges typically offer a user-friendly interface, a wide range of trading features, and the ability to deposit and withdraw funds using various payment methods.

Peer-to-Peer Marketplaces: These platforms enable direct transactions between individual users, bypassing intermediaries. Examples include LocalBitcoins, Paxful, and Bisq. These marketplaces offer more privacy and control, but may require more due diligence and may involve higher risks.

Bitcoin ATMs: These physical machines allow users to exchange cash for Bitcoin. They are becoming increasingly prevalent in many cities around the world, providing a convenient way to acquire Bitcoin.

After acquiring Bitcoin, you can hold it as a long-term investment or initiate trading activities.

Selling Bitcoin [2]

When you are ready to sell your Bitcoin, you can employ the same methods mentioned above in reverse order. This includes trading Bitcoin on an exchange, through a peer-to-peer marketplace, or utilizing a Bitcoin ATM.

Types of Exchanges

There are two primary types of Bitcoin exchanges:

Centralized Exchanges: These are the most prevalent form of Bitcoin exchanges, where a single entity operates as an intermediary between buyers and sellers. Centralized exchanges offer a wide range of features, such as advanced trading tools, liquidity, and user-friendly interfaces. However, they come with the risk of potential hacking or shutdown, as they hold control over users' funds.

Decentralized Exchanges: These operate on a blockchain network and lack a singular control point. Decentralized exchanges (DEXs) are more secure, as they do not hold users' funds, and transactions are conducted directly between wallets. However, they often have fewer features and may be less intuitive for some users.

Trading Strategies [3]

Traders employ various strategies when trading Bitcoin. Some of the most common include:

Buy and Hold (Hodling): This long-term strategy involves purchasing Bitcoin and holding it for an extended period, with the expectation that its value will appreciate over time.

Swing Trading: This approach involves buying and selling Bitcoin over shorter time frames, aiming to profit from price fluctuations. Swing traders may hold positions for days or weeks, seeking to capitalize on market trends.

Day Trading: Day traders execute multiple buy and sell orders within the same day, seeking to make numerous small profits by exploiting short-term price movements.

Technical Analysis: Traders may use various technical indicators, chart patterns, and other analytical tools to identify potential trading opportunities and make informed decisions.

Diversification: Some traders may choose to allocate their funds across different cryptocurrencies, reducing their exposure to the volatility of any single asset.

Regardless of the strategy, it is essential to conduct thorough research, understand the risks involved, and develop a well-planned approach to navigate the dynamic and volatile nature of the Bitcoin market.

1. https://www.forbes.com/advisor/investing/cryptocurrency/how-to-buy-bitcoin/
2. https://www.bankrate.com/investing/how-to-cash-out-crypto-bitcoin/#trade-one-crypto-for-another-and-then-cash-out
3. https://www.ig.com/en-ch/trading-strategies/the-5-crypto-trading-strategies-that-every-trader-needs-to-know-221123

Chapter 28

Bitcoin's Market Volatility: What Causes It and How to Navigate It

Bitcoin's market volatility is renowned for its rapid and sometimes substantial price fluctuations. This characteristic can pose challenges for investors seeking to manage risk, especially given the evolving regulatory landscape and the nascent state of the cryptocurrency market. In this chapter, we will delve into the factors contributing to Bitcoin's market volatility and guide navigating it.

Causes of Bitcoin's Market Volatility

a. Lack of Fundamental Value: Unlike traditional assets such as stocks or bonds, Bitcoin lacks intrinsic value. Its price is primarily determined by market demand and supply, making it susceptible to shifts in investor sentiment. This lack of a clear underlying valuation basis can exacerbate volatility as prices are primarily driven by speculation and perception rather than objective measures. [1]

b. Speculation: Bitcoin has attracted an influx of speculators aiming to capitalize on rapid price movements, further amplifying volatility. These speculative traders often engage in short-term trading strategies, causing sharp price swings as they enter and exit the market. [2]

c. Limited Market Size: Bitcoin's market capitalization is relatively small compared to conventional assets. As a result, substantial buy or sell orders can exert a disproportionate influence on its price, leading to more pronounced price movements. [3]

d. Regulatory Uncertainty: The absence of clear regulatory frameworks for cryptocurrencies has engendered uncertainty and apprehension among investors. Regulatory changes, such as the introduction of new rules or the crackdown on certain practices, can trigger significant price fluctuations as investors react to the perceived implications. [4]

e. News and Events: Significant news or events about Bitcoin, such as exchange breaches, regulatory crackdowns, or substantial institutional investments, can substantially influence its price trajectory. Investors often react quickly to these developments, causing abrupt price changes. [5]

f. Technological Factors: The underlying blockchain technology powering Bitcoin is constantly evolving, with new features and upgrades being introduced. Changes to the Bitcoin protocol or the emergence of competing cryptocurrencies can affect investor sentiment and contribute to price volatility. [6]

Tips for Navigating Bitcoin's Market Volatility

a. Diversify: Spreading investments across various assets and classes is pivotal in mitigating risk. Avoid concentrating all investments on a single support, as this can amplify the impact of Bitcoin's price swings on your portfolio.

b. Set Realistic Expectations: Recognize that Bitcoin's price is highly volatile and entails inherent risks. Establish reasonable expectations for potential returns, and be prepared to withstand significant price fluctuations.

c. Have a Long-Term Strategy: Consider adopting a long-term investment strategy that takes into account the potential risks and rewards of investing in Bitcoin. Avoid making decisions based on short-term price movements, as this can lead to emotional decision-making and suboptimal outcomes.

d. Stay Informed: Keep abreast of significant news and events about Bitcoin, including regulatory changes, technological developments, and major industry trends. Being well-informed can assist in anticipating potential price fluctuations and making more informed investment decisions.

e. Use Stop-Loss Orders: Employing stop-loss orders can help minimize potential losses by automatically triggering the sale of Bitcoin if it reaches a predefined price threshold. This can provide a measure of protection against sudden price drops.

f. Seek Professional Advice: Consider consulting a financial advisor or investment professional with expertise in cryptocurrencies. Their insights and guidance can be invaluable in navigating the volatile Bitcoin market and developing a well-informed investment strategy.

g. Utilize Risk Management Techniques: Explore advanced risk management strategies, such as options trading or hedging, to mitigate the impact of Bitcoin's volatility on your portfolio. These techniques can provide a layer of protection against adverse price movements.

In conclusion, while Bitcoin's market volatility presents a notable challenge for investors, careful planning and a long-term perspective can pave the way for successful navigation. By comprehending the factors contributing to price volatility and implementing a comprehensive set of strategies to mitigate risk, investors can position themselves to seize the potential rewards offered by this dynamic asset class.

1. https://aithority.com/guest-authors/bitcoin-has-no-intrinsic-value-then-what-gives-bitcoin-value/
2. https://medium.com/@bughinjacquesrenejean/is-bitcoin-a-speculative-bubble-4cc623a9f5bf

3. https://www.grandviewresearch.com/industry-analysis/bitcoin-market
4. https://mitsloan.mit.edu/ideas-made-to-matter/how-crypto-investors-behave-and-why-industry-needs-regulation
5. https://coinmarketcal.com/en/
6. https://www.ncbi.nlm.nih.gov/pmc/articles/PMC9204170/

Chapter 29

Approval of Bitcoin ETFs by the SEC

What Are the Benefits of ETFs for Bitcoin?

For those seeking to invest in Bitcoin, ETFs present a myriad of advantages, showcasing their allure through enhanced accessibility, diversified investment options, and reduced fees compared to conventional methods of directly owning Bitcoin.

One prominent benefit of utilizing ETFs for Bitcoin investments[1] lies in their seamless accessibility. By bypassing the intricacies associated with the secure acquisition and storage of Bitcoin, investors can effortlessly acquire and divest ETF shares via traditional brokerage accounts. This simplified approach broadens the horizons of Bitcoin investment, allowing a wider array of individuals to partake in this thriving market, unencumbered by potential barriers that would have otherwise hindered their participation.

The SEC's Decision to Approve Bitcoin ETF

The recent approval of Bitcoin ETFs by the Securities and Exchange Commission [2] (SEC) in the United States marks a momentous milestone in the recognition of cryptocurrencies within the traditional financial market. This groundbreaking decision signifies a significant step toward mainstream acceptance and integration of Bitcoin and other digital assets into established investment frameworks.

With the SEC's approval, a new era unfolds for cryptocurrencies, particularly Bitcoin, as it opens doors for broader adoption and inclusion within institutional investment strategies. These newly approved cryptocurrency ETFs are anticipated to attract the interest of institutional investors who were previously hesitant due to regulatory uncertainties surrounding digital assets.

This regulatory development not only sets a precedent for future approvals but also has the potential to shape the perception and trading of other digital assets within the financial markets. It signals a gradual evolution in the regulatory landscape for cryptocurrencies, paving the way for further advancements and opportunities in the realm of digital finance.

What Does This Mean for Bitcoin and the Cryptocurrency Market?

The SEC's approval of Bitcoin ETFs [3] is poised to have a transformative impact on Bitcoin and the broader cryptocurrency market, potentially leading to increased institutional investment, enhanced market liquidity, and improved price discovery mechanisms.

Following the SEC's decision, the inclusion of Bitcoin ETFs in the traditional financial system is expected to provide a stamp of credibility to the cryptocurrency, attracting a wave of new investors looking for exposure to the digital asset. The approval signals a maturing acceptance of digital assets in mainstream markets, paving the way for greater integration of cryptocurrencies into traditional investment portfolios.

This milestone could also contribute to a significant shift in investor sentiment toward Bitcoin, as more institutional players gain access to the asset class through regulated channels. The increased participation of established financial firms in the crypto space suggests a growing recognition of the long-term potential and value of cryptocurrencies.

Impact on Bitcoin's Price

The SEC's approval of Bitcoin ETFs has the potential to drive significant price movements [4] in the cryptocurrency market. Increased institutional investment and market participation can influence the valuation of Bitcoin and contribute to overall price stability.

As institutional investors enter the Bitcoin market through ETFs, we can anticipate a surge in trading activity and liquidity. This influx of participation may result in a more stable price trajectory for Bitcoin. However, in the short term, the market could experience heightened volatility. ETF approval announcements often spark speculative behavior among retail traders, leading to sudden price fluctuations.

It is worth noting that historically, regulatory approvals and official endorsements have had a positive impact on Bitcoin prices. Such approvals create anticipation for greater mainstream acceptance, attracting more capital inflows and solidifying Bitcoin's position as a valuable digital asset in the global financial landscape. Therefore, if the SEC grants approval for Bitcoin ETFs, it could signal a new era for the cryptocurrency.

Impact on Other Cryptocurrencies

The approval of Bitcoin ETFs is likely to send ripples across the cryptocurrency landscape, affecting the valuation and market sentiment of altcoins. As investors realign their portfolios to seize the expanding opportunities in the digital asset realm, altcoins may experience shifts in their fortunes.

This change in investor behavior is driven by the expectation of wider acceptance of cryptocurrencies, driven by the regulatory approval of Bitcoin ETFs. As Bitcoin, the dominant player in the market, garners institutional recognition and adoption, its influence permeates the entire cryptocurrency market. Altcoins, eager to distinguish themselves from the pioneering digital asset, often face heightened volatility and price fluctuations due to their close ties to Bitcoin's performance.

Impact on Institutional Investment

The SEC's approval of Bitcoin ETFs is poised to ignite a surge in institutional investment [5] within the cryptocurrency realm. With regulated ETF products providing a secure and accessible entry point, large financial institutions can now confidently venture into the world of digital assets.

The introduction of ETFs grants institutional investors a convenient avenue to allocate significant capital to Bitcoin. This influx of institutional participation has the potential to enhance market liquidity and stability. Furthermore, the approval of Bitcoin ETFs signifies a pivotal shift towards mainstream acceptance of cryptocurrencies in the traditional financial sector. As a result, we can expect to see diversified investment portfolios that include digital assets.

Compliance with regulations is a paramount concern for institutional players navigating this ever-evolving landscape. ETFs offer a structured framework that aligns with existing regulations, instilling a sense of confidence and legitimacy that encourages greater participation from institutional investors.

The strategic adoption of digital assets by established financial entities can be viewed as a forward-thinking move to diversify their portfolios and adapt to the changing investment landscape. By incorporating Bitcoin ETFs into their offerings, these institutions not only cater to the growing demand for exposure to cryptocurrencies but also position themselves as pioneers in the digital asset space.

Security Concerns

Investors in Bitcoin ETFs are rightfully concerned about security vulnerabilities and custodial risks associated with digital assets. The safekeeping of these assets and protection against cyber threats are crucial in maintaining the integrity of investment portfolios.

One of the main challenges in Bitcoin ETF security [6] is selecting the right custodial solutions that offer robust protection against potential breaches and unauthorized access. It is essential to prioritize cybersecurity best practices to safeguard digital assets from malicious attacks and data breaches. By implementing stringent asset protection measures, investors can mitigate risks associated with theft and fraud, providing them with a greater sense of security and peace of mind.

Ensuring the security of Bitcoin ETFs is of paramount importance. Investors should carefully consider the custodial solutions and storage mechanisms employed by ETF providers to ensure the safekeeping of their digital assets. By prioritizing security measures and staying informed about the latest advancements in cybersecurity, investors can mitigate risks and confidently navigate the world of Bitcoin ETF investments.

1. https://www.ulam.io/blog/understanding-bitcoin-etfs-risks-and-opportunities
2. https://www.theguardian.com/technology/2024/jan/11/bitcoin-etf-approved-sec-explained-meaning-securities-regulator-tweet
3. https://apnews.com/article/bitcoin-exchange-traded-funds-etf-sec-59a5bb81ab891af57a1bd1765024144f
4. https://economictimes.indiatimes.com/markets/cryptocurrency/bitcoin-etfs-the-gateway-to-mainstream-crypto-adoption/articleshow/107004315.cms?from=mdr
5. https://www.lexology.com/library/detail.aspx?g=60f2b232-d2eb-4145-9875-62a5b49ed18d
6. https://www.halborn.com/blog/post/bitcoin-etf-security-risks-a-guide-for-issuers-and-buyers

Chapter 30

Bitcoin and Cryptocurrency Innovations: What Lies Ahead?

In this era of escalating digitalization, the hunger for groundbreaking technologies and solutions knows no bounds. Bitcoin and its cryptocurrency cohorts have already shaken the foundations of conventional financial systems. Yet, what vistas of innovation loom on the horizon?

Pioneering Scalability Solutions

At the forefront of challenges confronting Bitcoin and its ilk is the issue of scalability [1]. The influx of users begets a languid pace and augmented costs in transactions. Many scaling remedies grace the drawing board, with the Lightning Network leading the charge. This ingenious network facilitates expeditious and cost-effective off-chain transactions. Additionally, advancements in second-layer scaling solutions, such as the Liquid Network and Plasma, promise to boost Bitcoin's transaction throughput while preserving its decentralized ethos.

Veiling Transactions in Privacy's Mantle

While Bitcoin transactions cloak themselves in a veneer of technical anonymity, they are not impervious to scrutiny on the blockchain. Enterprising minds have birthed privacy-boosting panaceas, exemplified by CoinJoin [2] and ZeroLink [3]. These tools amalgamate multiple transactions, fashioning a labyrinth for would-be sleuths to navigate. The emergence of privacy-centric cryptocurrencies, like Monero and Zcash, further ushers in a new era of financial confidentiality, catering to those who value the sanctity of their transactions.

The Dawn of Decentralized Finance (DeFi)

DeFi stands as an uncharted frontier, endeavoring to emancipate conventional financial services—lending, borrowing, and trading—from centralization's clutches. The Ethereum blockchain has already birthed several bastions of DeFi, but Bitcoin harbors the potential to serve as a fertile ground for decentralized financial endeavors. Projects like Sovryn [4] and RenVM [5] are leveraging Bitcoin's network to create decentralized exchange platforms and cross-chain asset bridges, broadening the scope of DeFi beyond Ethereum.

Central Bank Digital Currencies (CBDCs): A Tectonic Shift

The echelons of central banking entertain the notion of minting their digital currencies. Albeit tethered to a central authority, these currencies proffer the allure of swifter and more economic transactions—a paradigm shift in the financial landscape. The advent of CBDCs [6] could potentially spur further innovation, as cryptocurrencies adapt to coexist and interoperate with these state-backed digital assets, forging a new era of hybrid finance.

Bridging Blockchains: The Quest for Interoperability

The current milieu finds cryptocurrencies ensconced within their respective blockchains, an archipelago of isolated value. Enterprising minds rally under the banner of interoperability, with the Polkadot network spearheading this charge. Here, blockchains commune, fostering a network of fluid value exchange. Projects like Cosmos [7] and Avalanche [8] also aim to bridge the gap between disparate blockchain ecosystems, ushering in an era of seamless asset transfer and cross-chain integration.

A Verdant Horizon: Green Mining Endeavors

In the crucible of critique, Bitcoin's voracious appetite for energy and its ecological footprint is scrutinized. Enterprising projects champion eco-conscious mining, harnessing renewable founts of energy to fuel mining operations—a beacon of hope for a sustainable future. Initiatives like the Bitcoin Mining Council [9] and the Crypto Climate Accord [10] are driving the industry towards more environmentally responsible practices, exploring innovative solutions such as nuclear energy, geothermal power, and waste heat recovery.

Steadfast Anchors: The Rise of Stablecoins

In a realm where Bitcoin's price charters tempestuous waters, stablecoins emerge as a stalwart bulwark. Engineered to tether their value to a stable benchmark—say, the US dollar—they promise a haven of stability and predictability in a turbulent sea of volatility. The proliferation of stablecoins, from the likes of Tether [11] and USD Coin [12] to the emergence of central bank-backed digital currencies, has paved the way for their integration into decentralized finance ecosystems, serving as a bridge between traditional finance and the crypto realm.

Scripting the Future: Smart Contracts Take Center Stage

Smart contracts stand as the vanguard of self-executing agreements, their terms etched in the hallowed halls of code. Bitcoin's scripting vernacular already lays the rudimentary foundation, but platforms like Ethereum vault beyond, offering a canvas for the most intricate of contractual symphonies. The continued evolution of smart contract capabilities [13], including the integration of oracles, multi-signature functionality, and advanced programming languages, promises to revolutionize the way we engage in a myriad of industries, from finance and supply chain management to real estate and beyond.

In summation, the world of cryptocurrencies unfurls in perpetual metamorphosis, promising an ever-expanding repertoire of inventive solutions and applications. From scalability saviors to decentralized finance and verdant mining initiatives, the panorama is boundless. The trajectory of Bitcoin and its brethren promises to redefine our financial infrastructure and revolutionize the very essence of value transference—the future beckons, rife with possibilities.

1. https://financefeeds.com/exsat-unveiled-pioneering-the-future-of-bitcoin-scalability-and-interoperability-with-layer-2-solutions/
2. https://www.coinjoins.org/
3. https://www.coinbureau.com/review/bitcoin-tumbling-zerolink-will-hide-coins/
4. https://sovryn.app/
5. https://www.gemini.com/cryptopedia/ren-token-and-renvm-crypto-platform
6. https://www.imf.org/en/Topics/fintech/central-bank-digital-currency/virtual-handbook
7. https://cosmos.network/
8. https://www.avax.network/
9. https://bitcoinminingcouncil.com/
10. https://cryptoclimate.org/
11. https://tether.to/en/
12. https://www.circle.com/en/usdc
13. https://www.ibm.com/topics/smart-contracts

Glossary

Bitcoin: A decentralized digital currency that enables instant peer-to-peer transactions without the need for intermediaries.

Cryptocurrency: A digital or virtual currency secured by cryptography, typically operating on a decentralized network using blockchain technology.

Blockchain: A distributed ledger technology that records transactions across multiple computers in a way that is immutable, transparent, and secure.

Decentralization: The distribution of control and decision-making across a network of nodes, rather than relying on a central authority.

Wallet: Software or hardware used to store, send, and receive cryptocurrencies. Wallets can be hot (connected to the internet) or cold (offline for increased security).

Mining: The process of validating and adding transactions to the blockchain through computational power, typically rewarded with newly minted coins and transaction fees.

Hash: A cryptographic function that converts an input (data) into a fixed-size string of characters, used in blockchain to secure and verify transactions.

Node: A computer or device connected to a blockchain network that maintains a copy of the ledger and participates in transaction validation and consensus.

Fork: A divergence in the blockchain, resulting in two or more versions of the blockchain with a shared history up to a certain point.

Consensus: The process by which participants in a blockchain network agree on the validity of transactions and the state of the ledger.

Altcoin: Any cryptocurrency other than Bitcoin, often used to refer to alternative cryptocurrencies launched after Bitcoin's success.

Token: A digital asset representing ownership or access rights, often built on existing blockchains like Ethereum.

Smart Contract: Self-executing contracts with the terms of the agreement directly written into code, automatically enforced on the blockchain.

Distributed Ledger: A type of database spread across multiple nodes, where each node maintains a copy of the ledger and updates occur in a synchronized manner.

Immutable: Refers to the inability to change or alter data once it has been recorded on the blockchain, ensuring data integrity and trustworthiness.

ICO (Initial Coin Offering): A fundraising method for new cryptocurrency projects, where investors purchase tokens in exchange for established cryptocurrencies like Bitcoin or Ethereum.

Exchange: A platform where cryptocurrencies can be traded for other digital assets or fiat currencies.

Private Key/Public Key: Pair of cryptographic keys used to secure transactions on the blockchain. The private key is kept secret and used to sign transactions, while the public key is shared and used to verify signatures.

Wallet Address: A unique identifier used to send and receive cryptocurrencies, derived from the public key.

Double Spending: The risk of spending the same digital currency more than once, is typically prevented by blockchain's consensus mechanism.

Halving: An event that occurs approximately every four years in Bitcoin's protocol, reducing the reward for mining new blocks by half, designed to control inflation and ensure scarcity.

Satoshis: The smallest unit of Bitcoin, equal to one hundred millionth of a Bitcoin (0.00000001 BTC), is named after Bitcoin's pseudonymous creator, Satoshi Nakamoto.

Whale: A term used to describe individuals or entities that hold significant amounts of cryptocurrency, capable of influencing market prices with their transactions.

Hash Rate: The speed at which a mining machine operates, measured in hashes per second, indicating the computational power dedicated to securing the blockchain.

Wallet Seed: A random sequence of words used to generate a deterministic wallet, allowing users to restore their wallet and access funds if the original wallet is lost or damaged.

Block Height: A numerical value representing the number of blocks in the blockchain, used to measure the progression of the blockchain.

Cold Storage: Storing cryptocurrencies offline, typically in hardware wallets or paper wallets, to protect them from hacking or theft.

Gas: The unit used to measure the computational effort required to execute operations on the Ethereum blockchain, paid by users to execute smart contracts and transactions.

DeFi (Decentralized Finance): Financial services built on blockchain technology that operates without intermediaries, enabling greater accessibility, transparency, and efficiency.

Stablecoin: A type of cryptocurrency designed to maintain a stable value, often pegged to a fiat currency or commodity, reducing volatility.

References

The First Step: Tracing the Origins of Bitcoin with the Genesis Transaction.
https://genesislabcom.medium.com/the-first-step-tracing-the-origins-of-bitcoin-with-the-genesis-transaction-a740e2696611

What To Know About Cryptocurrency and Scams
https://consumer.ftc.gov/articles/what-know-about-cryptocurrency-and-scams

Understanding Non-Fungible Tokens (NFTs) and Cryptocurrencies
https://www.mcallisterbrewing.com/post/understanding-non-fungible-tokens-nfts-and-cryptocurrencies

Bitcoin: A Peer-to-Peer Electronic Cash System
https://bitcoin.org/bitcoin.pdf

Commodity Futures Trading Commission
https://www.cftc.gov/

Bitcoin in the economics and finance literature: a survey
https://www.ncbi.nlm.nih.gov/pmc/articles/PMC8174543/

On Bitcoin: A Study in Applied Metaphysics
https://academic.oup.com/pq/article/73/3/783/7085492

Towards Reference Architecture for Cryptocurrencies: Bitcoin Architectural Analysis
https://www.researchgate.net/publication/286056422_Towards_Reference_Architecture_for_Cryptocurrencies_Bitcoin_Architectural_Analysis

Price Fluctuations and the Use of Bitcoin: An Empirical Inquiry
https://www.ecb.europa.eu/pub/conferences/shared/pdf/retpaym_150604/polasik_paper.pdf

Bitcoin's Academic Pedigree
https://queue.acm.org/detail.cfm?id=3136559

The Bitcoin as a Virtual Commodity: Empirical Evidence and Implications
https://www.frontiersin.org/articles/10.3389/frai.2020.00021/full

Bitcoin: A First Legal Analysis - with reference to German and US-American law
https://www.zar.kit.edu/DATA/veroeffentlichungen/237_BTC_final_camready_437e610.pdf

Investigating the Adoption Factors of Cryptocurrencies
https://journals.sagepub.com/doi/full/10.1177/2158244021998704

The brutal truth about Bitcoin
https://www.brookings.edu/articles/the-brutal-truth-about-bitcoin/

Cryptocurrency as an investment or speculation: a bibliometric review study
https://www.emerald.com/insight/content/doi/10.1108/BAJ-07-2022-0008/full/html

Tracing Knowledge Diffusion Trajectories in Scholarly Bitcoin Research: Co-Word and Main Path Analyses
https://www.mdpi.com/1911-8074/16/8/355

Is the Bitcoin market efficient? A literature review
https://www.scielo.org.mx/scielo.php?script=sci_arttext&pid=S2448-66552021000300167

'DON'T TRUST, VERIFY': FIXING THE PROBLEMS WITH ACADEMIC RESEARCH ON BITCOIN
https://bitcoinmagazine.com/culture/fixing-academic-research-on-bitcoin

In digital we trust Bitcoin discourse, digital currencies, and decentralized network fetishism
https://www.nature.com/articles/s41599-018-0065-0

A place next to Satoshi: foundations of blockchain and cryptocurrency research in business and economics
https://link.springer.com/article/10.1007/s11192-020-03492-8

Understanding Bitcoin: Cryptography, engineering, and economics.
https://onlinelibrary.wiley.com/doi/pdf/10.1002/9781119019138.biblio

The use of cryptocurrency in business
https://www2.deloitte.com/us/en/pages/audit/articles/corporates-using-crypto.html

Bitcoin – a Currency or an Asset?
https://core.ac.uk/download/pdf/288306861.pdf

Bitcoin: Economics, Technology, and Governance
https://www.aeaweb.org/articles?id=10.1257/jep.29.2.213

BITCOIN: ITS INFLUENCE ON THE GLOBAL WORLD AND ITS RELATIONSHIP WITH THE STOCK EXCHANGE
https://www.redalyc.org/journal/5717/571763394004/html/

A bibliometric review of cryptocurrencies: how have they grown?
https://jfin-swufe.springeropen.com/articles/10.1186/s40854-021-00306-5

Cryptocurrencies, Digital Dollars, and the Future of Money

https://www.cfr.org/backgrounder/cryptocurrencies-digital-dollars-and-future-money

Bitcoin, Blockchain, and FinTech: A Systematic Review and Case Studies in the Supply Chain
https://papers.ssrn.com/sol3/papers.cfm?abstract_id=3281148

Bitcoin Pricing, Adoption, and Usage: Theory and Evidence
https://www.gsb.stanford.edu/faculty-research/working-papers/bitcoin-pricing-adoption-usage-theory-evidence

Is Bitcoin a decentralized payment mechanism?
https://www.cambridge.org/core/journals/journal-of-institutional-economics/article/is-bitcoin-a-decentralized-payment-mechanism/16CA6A2E4440BB4E715E3E745A34C355

Bitcoin's energy consumption is underestimated: A market dynamics approach
https://www.sciencedirect.com/science/article/pii/S2214629620302966

The crypto ecosystem: key elements and risks
https://www.bis.org/publ/othp72.pdf

Bitcoin: An Innovative Alternative Digital Currency
https://repository.uclawsf.edu/hastings_science_technology_law_journal/vol4/iss1/3/

Climate Impacts of Bitcoin Mining in the U.S.

https://ceepr.mit.edu/wp-content/uploads/2023/06/MIT-CEEPR-WP-2023-11.pdf

CRYPTOCURRENCY: A MINE OF CONTROVERSIES
https://www.scielo.br/j/jistm/a/3qvYLtmcg6MGw9P7x733RZb/

www.ingramcontent.com/pod-product-compliance
Lightning Source LLC
Chambersburg PA
CBHW052210220526
45471CB00004B/1895